SCONES

PRESERVED GINGER SCONES.

½ lb. flour (one breakfastcup)
1 oz. butter
¼ teaspoon salt
¼ teaspoon sugar
1 teaspoon Baking Powder
Preserved Ginger
Milk and water to mix

Sift baking powder and salt with flour, rub in butter, mix to a stiff dough, turn out on board, cut in two equal parts, roll out, spread one-half with thinly-cut ginger, place the other half on top, cut in squares, brush over the milk, and bake in quick oven.

CINNAMON SCONES.

1 lb. flour
3 teaspoonfuls Baking Powder
2 ozs. butter
1 egg
2 teaspoonfuls ground cinnamon
Milk to mix, sugar to taste, salt to taste

Make a light scone mixture, roll out quickly, sprinkle cinnamon, fold in three, roll lightly to required thickness, cut to shape, bake in quick oven.

GIRDLE SCONES.

3 level breakfastcups flour
3 teaspoonfuls Baking Powder
Salt to taste

Mix with large cup of milk and water, divide dough into half, roll out, and cut 4 scones from each. Cook on hot girdle.

YORKSHIRE TEA SCONES.

¾ lb. flour (or 1½ large cups)
1 oz. butter (or a tablespoonful)
1 dessertspoonful sugar
½ cup milk
2 teaspoonfuls Baking Powder
1 egg

Put butter into a saucepan, when dissolved put in the milk, and make warm; place sugar in a basin, and pour on the warm milk. Then place flour in mixing bowl, and mix in Baking Powder, make a well in centre, and drop in the egg, then pour on milk and mix well. The paste should be thin, roll and cut into shapes, place on hot floured oven shelf, and bake in hot oven 10 minutes.

CARRAWAY BISCUITS.

1½ lbs. of flour
½ lb. butter
¾ lb. Sugar
2 eggs
2 teaspoonfuls Baking Powder
2 ozs. currants
2 ozs. candied peel
1 teaspoonful carraway seeds
Little milk

Rub the butter into the flour, add the sugar, baking powder, cleaned currants, carraway seeds, and finely-chopped candied peel. Mix to a stiff paste with the well-beaten eggs, and a little milk. Roll out on a floured board, cut into shapes, and bake in quick oven.

"UP-TO-DATE" BROWN SCONES.

2 breakfastcups of wheatmeal
1 breakfastcup plain flour
3 teaspoonfuls Baking Powder
3 ozs. butter (or lard)
2 heaped dessertspoonfuls sugar
1 egg
Large cup milk. Salt to taste

Mix the wheatmeal, flour, sugar and Baking Powder, then rub in butter (or lard), beat the egg and milk together, and make into stiff dough. Roll and cut into shapes, place on hot floured oven shelf, and bake in quick oven.

SULTANA SCONES.

2 breakfastcups flour
3 moderate teaspoonfuls Baking Powder
2 tablespoonfuls butter
2 dessertspoonfuls sugar
1 egg, half pint milk, salt to taste
1 oz. sultanas or currants

Rub the butter (or lard) into the flour, and add the sugar, sultanas, and baking powder. Beat the egg, and add the milk to it, then mix all together to a wet dough. Roll out on floured board; cut into shapes, and bake in moderate oven 20 minutes.

SCOTCH SCONES.

2 breakfastcups flour
2 heaped teaspoons Baking Powder
2 ozs. butter
1 cup milk
Salt to taste

Mix flour and baking powder, then rub in 2 ozs. butter, half a pint milk, mix quickly, roll and cut into shapes, bake in hot oven.

PLAIN SCONES.

1 breakfastcup flour (piled up)
1½ teaspoons Baking Powder
1 oz. butter (or lard)
1 teaspoon sugar
1 egg

Rub butter (or lard) into flour, then add other dry ingredients, beat egg with little water, mix all into dough. Bake as usual, quick oven. If made without the egg, use milk in place of water.

TIP

To soften scones always turn out on clean towel, and cover them with the ends.

BREAD and ROLLS

COFFEE ROLLS.

3 breakfastcups flour
2 tablespoonfuls butter
3 teaspoonfuls Baking Powder
1 egg
½ pint milk, or more if needed.
1 tablespoonful sugar

Mix baking powder and flour together. Beat butter and sugar to a cream; add egg (beaten), then milk, shape dough oblong, and cut. Make dough same consistency as for scones.

DATE ROLLS.

1 lb. flour (or 2 breakfastcups)
4 ozs. sugar
2 eggs
4 ozs. butter
2 teaspoonfuls Baking Powder
½ lb. dates or sultanas chopped
Milk to mix, salt a pinch, cinnamon

Rub butter into flour, add all dry ingredients, beat egg till frothy, mix all together to a stiff paste, turn out on a board, form into a roll, and cut in equal parts, put on cold, greased, and floured oven tray, and put in quick oven; when nearly done brush over with hot water, and sprinkle liberally with cinnamon and sugar; return to oven to dry.

MILK ROLLS.

2 breakfastcups flour
2 tablespoonfuls butter
1 breakfastcup milk
2 heaped teaspoons Baking Powder

Mix into a stiff dough, roll into oblong shape, cut into pieces, brush over with milk, and bake about 20 minutes.

COTTAGE LOAF.

2 lbs. flour
2 moderate dessertspoonfuls of Baking Powder
½ teaspoonful salt
1 pint milk

Mix the baking powder and salt thoroughly with the flour, and work into light dough with milk. Bake in quick oven.

AERATED BREAD.

To every cup of flour add a heaped teaspoonful of Baking Powder, with a pinch of salt, thoroughly mix while in a dry state, then pour on gradually about half pint of cold water or milk; mix quickly but thoroughly into dough of the usual consistence. Do not knead it more than necessary to mix it perfectly. Make into small loaves, and place immediately in quick oven. (When fully risen open door to let out the steam just a second).

BROWN BREAD.

2 breakfastcups of wheatmeal
1 small cup flour
1 teaspoon sugar
2 heaped teaspoons Baking Powder
1 small teaspoon salt
1 tablespoonful butter
1 breakfastcup milk and water

Mix all the ingredients with the milk and water into dough, turn out and flatten with hand, inch thick, cut four lines across the top, and prick with fork. Bake about 20 minutes.

PUDDINGS

RICE PUDDING (Without Eggs).

Stir sufficient rice in boiling water, let boil quarter of an hour, then drain water off, stirring into the boiled rice a cupful of milk and dessertspoonful of sugar. Make a custard (see direction for Custard, page 41), put the rice into a dish, mix thoroughly with the custard while hot. Grate nutmeg on top; bake as usual.

SAGO PUDDING (Without Eggs).

Stir sufficient sago in boiling water, let boil 15 minutes, then drain water off, stir into the sago a cupful of milk and dessertspoonful sugar; make custard (see direction for Custard, page 41); pour the stewed sago into a dish, mix well with the custard while hot. Grate nutmeg on top; bake as usual.

YORKSHIRE PUDDING.

1 heaped breakfastcup flour
1 pint milk, good measure
½ teaspoon salt
3 eggs
1 tablespoon dripping

Sift flour into a basin, sprinkle salt over it, and make a hole in the middle. Break each egg separately, and stir gradually in, add sufficient milk with wooden spoon until thick batter, then add and mix remainder of milk, and allow the batter to stand for half-an-hour. Place the dripping into a baking dish, make quite hot, and pour in batter; bake slowly for half-hour. A layer of raisins put in bottom of tin before pouring in batter makes a nice raisin Batter Pudding; try this.

BREAD AND BUTTER PUDDING (Without Eggs).

Slice sufficient white or brown bread (stale) to fill a good-sized pie dish, and spread each slice thinly with butter. Grease the dish, then lay in the slices, sprinkling some currants, sultanas, and sliced candied peel between each layer, adding a little sugar and spice also. Then moisten the bread with a cup of milk. Prepare a pint custard (see direction for Custard, page 41), and pour over while hot, grate nutmeg on; bake as usual.

RITA'S APPLE PUDDING.

Mix thoroughly a teaspoon of Baking Powder with a breakfastcup of flour. Beat 2 eggs well, add 1 gill of milk, and a tablespoon of butter, beat all together 15 minutes. Place 2 inches of stewed apples (sweetened) in a pie dish. Pour in batter, and bake in quick oven; serve hot.

RASPBERRY PUDDING.

¼ lb. butter
¼ cupful sugar
2 eggs
1 teaspoonful Baking Powder
2 tablespoonfuls raspberry jam
1 breakfastcup flour

MODE.—Beat butter and sugar to a cream, add eggs (well beaten), then the flour, baking powder and jam; put into a buttered basin, and steam 2½ hours.

DATE PUDDING.

3 ozs. butter
6 ozs. flour
2 or 3 eggs
1 small teaspoon Baking Powder
4 ozs. sugar
4 ozs. dates
3 tablespoons milk
1 teaspoon lemon juice

MODE.—Beat butter and sugar to a cream, add eggs, and beat well. Then add milk, dates (chopped up fine), lemon juice, and last sift in the flour and baking powder mixed. Steam 2 hours in a buttered mould.

COCONUT CUSTARD.

Put small teacupful of desiccated coconut in pie-dish, then make a pint custard of 2 eggs, and pint of milk, with two dessertspoonfuls sugar. Pour over coconut, and bake as usual.

FRUIT PUDDING.

1 small cup sugar
2 breakfastcups flour
1 tablespoonful butter
2 eggs
2 teaspoonfuls Baking Powder
¾ cup milk (or more)

Beat butter and sugar to a cream, add eggs (beaten) and milk. Mix flour and baking powder together, and add to mixture. Grease two small dishes, fill half full of fresh fruit, pour over the batter; bake 1 hour.

AMERICAN PUDDING.

4 apples
½ pint milk
2 eggs
1 tablespoon flour
½ nutmeg
1 tablespoon minced suet
½ teaspoon Baking Powder
Sugar, sweeten to taste

Core and halve the apples, beat eggs, add flour, baking powder and milk. Grease a pie dish; lay the apples in (cut part down), pour the mixture over, then sprinkle in the minced suet, and grate nutmeg on top. Bake moderate half-hour.

DOMINION PUDDING.

1 breakfastcup flour
½ breakfastcup sugar
1 tablespoonful butter
1 egg
½ cupful sweet milk
1 teaspoon Baking Powder

Rub butter into flour and Baking Powder, add sugar, beat egg and milk together, and mix all into batter. Place some raisins at bottom of mould or basin, pour batter over, and steam for 1¼ hours.

BEEF STEAK PUDDING.

½ lb. bread crumbs
½ lb. flour
1 teaspoonful Baking Powder
1 lb. of steak
½ lb. suet
3 kidneys
Seasoning

Mix crumbs, flour, suet, salt to taste, and baking powder, with enough cold water to make stiff paste. Roll out and line a basin, leaving a small hole at the bottom of paste. Cut steak up and dredge with flour. Cut kidney small; add pepper and seasoning; cover with a thick layer of paste, and boil about 3 hours.

ROLLED FRENCH PUDDING.

Roll out a nice suet crust as for rolly poly, scatter over some chopped figs, dates, apple or lemon juice, finely chopped candied peel, breadcrumbs, golden syrup, ground ginger, and nutmeg, little pieces of butter here and there, roll up, secure ends, tie in cloth, and boil about 2 hours; put pudding into boiling water.

SUET DUMPLINGS.

1 teacupful flour
2 tablespoonfuls chopped suet
Cold water
pepper and salt to taste
½ teaspoon Baking Powder
1 dessertspoonful chopped parsley

Mix all the dry ingredients, rubbing suet into the flour, and make all into stiff paste with cold water. Cut and roll into balls, covering the outsides with flour, which prevents breaking. When ready, drop them into the stew, which must be boiling slowly, and cook for half-hour longer.

APPLE DUMPLINGS.

3 ozs. flour
½ teaspoon Baking Powder
3 apples
3 ozs. suet
3 ozs. breadcrumbs
¼ teaspoon salt
3 dessertspoonfuls sugar

Prepare the apples, make a paste of flour, suet, breadcrumbs, add baking powder, salt, and water to mix. Place a piece of paste round each apple, put dessertspoonful sugar in each, then cover the top. Put dumplings loose into pan of boiling water, when they come to surface give them ½ hour.

BAKED JAM ROLL.

½ lb. flour
4 ozs. dripping (or lard or butter)
Salt a little
½ teaspoon Baking Powder
½ teaspoon Sugar (fine)
Water to mix

Beat butter (or dripping) to a cream, add all other ingredients, and sufficient water to make a dough, roll out into shape, and spread with apricot or raspberry jam, sliced apples, plums, or any fruit desired could be substituted for jam. Put in a baking dish; bake in moderate oven.

HENDY PUDDING.

1 cup suet (chopped)
2 breakfastcups flour
¼ breakfastcup sugar
2 teaspoons Baking Powder (heaped)
Jam, water to mix

Mix all dry ingredients with water to a stiff dough, which divide into three, place alternately in greased basin a layer of dough, then jam, steam 3 hours. Serve with sweet or jam sauce.

BAKED APPLE DUMPLINGS.

1 lb. flour (or 2 breakfastcups)
½ lb. butter (or dripping)
½ teaspoon Baking Powder
Water to mix

Pare and core the apples, fill cavity with sugar and nutmeg, roll each separately in paste, put in baking dish, and quarter cover with hot water containing half cup sugar, one ounce of butter, one tablespoonful of Golden Syrup. Baste frequently, allow three-quarters of an hour to bake, try with skewer; serve with custard or cream.

CHRISTMAS PLUM PUDDING.

¾ lb. flour (or 1½ breakfastcups)
2 heaped teaspoonfuls Baking Powder
2 ozs. stale bread crumbs
1½ lb. suet
2 lbs. raisins
1 lb. currants
6 eggs
10 ozs. sugar (brown)
¼ lb. almonds
½ lb. mixed candied peel
Salt and spice to taste

Mix ingredients well together, and add 6 eggs well beaten, and three-quarters of a pint of milk; divide into two, and boil 8 hours, or four, and boil 6 hours.

DOUGHNUTS.

3½ breakfastcups flour
1 breakfastcup sugar
½ breakfastcup butter
4 eggs
1 cup milk
3 teaspoonfuls Baking Powder
½ teaspoonful salt

Beat sugar and eggs together in a separate basin, rub butter into flour, add salt and baking powder, mix well, then mix flour with the eggs and sugar, roll out, cut into rounds, and fry in hot lard; serve hot.

PASTRIES

MINCE PIES.

INGREDIENTS.—Mince meat, a sufficiency, and puff or short paste Recipes (see below).

Roll out the paste to a suitable thickness, line with it the patty pans, previously well buttered; put in each sufficient mince meat, make lids of paste, cover over, press lightly at the edges, neatly trim round with a knife, and bake in a moderately quick oven. When done, sprinkle with powdered white sugar.

MINCE MEAT.

2 lbs. apples (pared and cored)
2 lbs. raisins (stoned)
2 lbs. currants
2 lbs. suet (chopped fine)
¾ lb. mixed candied peel (chopped)
½ lb. sugar
½ pint brandy (or 1 breakfastcup)
¼ pint sherry (or ½ breakfastcup)
1 small nutmeg (grated)
1 dessertspoonful powdered cinnamon
1 dessertspoonful salt
The juice of two small oranges
The juice of two small lemons
The peel of one each grated

Put apples and raisins through mincer, then mix with all other ingredients well together, put into jars, with piece of paper on top dipped in brandy, then cover.

PLAIN PUFF PASTRY.

½ lb. flour
7 ozs. butter
½ teaspoonful Baking Powder
Water to mix

MODE.—Place the flour on a pastry-board with the butter, chop the butter into the flour with a knife, then put into a basin, add baking powder, and sufficient water to make a soft dough. Roll out several times.

SHORT PASTRY.

1 breakfastcup flour, pinch salt
4 ozs. butter or lard
½ teaspoonful Baking Powder
Water to mix

MODE.—Rub the butter into the flour, add salt, baking powder, and water a little at a time to make a firm dough. Roll out to required thickness.

YORKSHIRE CHEESE CAKES.

1 teacup curds
1 oz. butter
1 oz. sugar
1 egg
1 tablespoon currants

MODE.—Cream butter and sugar, mix with the curds, mix all ingredients together. Fill patty-pans, lined with pastry.

To prepare the curd, boil 2 quarts of milk, and as it rises pour in either ½ pint of vinegar or buttermilk to turn it to curds. Draw the pan to side of the fire, let it stand 5 minutes, then strain through a sieve.

Pastry requires a hot oven; if it contains baking powder—must be baked at once.

APPLE SANDWICH.

½ lb. butter
1 lb. flour
2 teaspoonfuls Baking Powder
Mince 2 or 3 apples
1 cupful clean currants
1 piece of peel
1 dessertspoonful cinnamon
1 lemon
1 egg
2 tablespoons sugar

MODE.—Rub butter into flour, then add baking powder, make into a firm dough with water. Roll out to required thickness; mince all other ingredients together, and mix in egg last. Place mince between pastry, and bake.

CORNISH PASTY.

¼ lb. pastry
1 teacupful raw potato
1 teacupful raw meat
A small piece of onion chopped fine
½ teaspoonful salt
¼ teaspoonful pepper
3 tablespoonfuls cold water or gravy

Mix all ingredients together on a plate, roll pastry into an oval shape, put the mixture on the paste, wet the edges on the top, and prick well. Brush over a little egg or milk, and bake in a hot oven for about half-an-hour.

A GOOD PIE CRUST.

4 breakfastcups flour
2 heaped teaspoonfuls Baking Powder
1 level teaspoon salt
1 lb. butter (lard or dripping may be used)

Mix well together, then add 2 cups of water, and roll out. This makes light paste for pies, tarts, custard, etc.

CAKES AND BUNS

RASPBERRY DELIGHTS.

2 tablespoonfuls sugar
1 egg
2 tablespoonfuls butter
½ teaspoonful Baking Powder
1 teaspoonful flour
1 tablespoonful Custard Powder

MODE.—Cream butter and sugar together, add the egg; mix flour, baking, and custard powder together, and add by degrees to mixture. Place in greased patty-tins on cold oven shelf, and bake ten minutes. When nearly baked, place a teaspoonful of raspberry jam on each, and then bake a little longer.

ENGLISH QUEEN CAKES.

4 eggs
Their weight in butter, sugar and flour
1 teaspoon Baking Powder
4 ozs. currants
Flavouring to taste

Beat butter and sugar to a cream, then beat in eggs. Mix currants with flour and baking powder, and add to mixture. Bake in hot oven.

CHELSEA BUNS.

2 breakfastcups flour
2 heaped teaspoons Baking Powder
2 tablespoonfuls sugar
2 tablespoonfuls butter
1 egg
Spice, and milk to mix

Rub all dry ingredients together, mix with milk to desired paste, roll out, cover with spice, and sugar, and bake as usual.

ALMOND FINGERS.

1 breakfastcup of flour
¼ lb. butter
2 ozs. sugar
1 egg
1 teaspoon Baking Powder

Beat butter and sugar to a cream, add yolk of egg, and beat well. Mix flour and baking powder together, and add to mixture with the hand. Paste must be very stiff. Roll out thin. Make the icing with the white of the egg, spread on top of paste. Place chopped almonds on. Cut into fingers; bake moderate oven.

RICH PLUM CAKE.

Take ½ lb. butter, and ½ lb. sugar, beat these well together with the hand to a cream, add 4 eggs, one at a time, beat well into the butter and sugar, lightly mix in 2 breakfastcups of flour previously mixed with one heaped teaspoon of Baking Powder, then lightly mix in ½ lb. sultanas. Bake at once thoroughly in fairly quick oven.

BUFFALO CAKE.

1¼ breakfastcups flour
¼ lb. butter
2 eggs
¾ breakfastcup sugar
2 teaspoonfuls Baking Powder

Cream butter and sugar, add eggs beaten, mix flour and baking powder, and add to mixture, then enough milk to make thin. Cook in sponge sandwich tins. Put together with lemon honey or raspberry jam. Icing on top.

SMALL CAKES (Without Eggs).

3 ozs. butter (or dripping)
3 ozs. sugar
½ lb. flour (or 1 breakfastcup)
1 teaspoonful ground ginger
1 heaped teaspoonful Egg Powder
Milk to mix about ¼ pint.

Soften butter or dripping if very hard, add sugar and beat to a cream. Slightly warm the milk, and beat it in by degrees. Stir in lightly the flour previously sifted with the Egg powder, ground ginger, and half a saltspoon of salt, drop in spoonfuls on a cold baking tray, sprinkle a little sugar over, and bake in hot oven for about ten minutes. The mixture for these and all eggless cakes must be fairly firm, and the spoonfuls piled high on the baking tray.

ELSIE'S FINGERS.

¼ lb. butter
3 ozs. sugar
2 small cups flour
1½ teaspoonfuls Baking Powder
1 egg

Beat butter and sugar, add egg and flour mixed with baking powder, roll small pieces between the hands, dip in sugar, and put on cold tray; bake in moderate oven till slightly brown.

PIKELETS.

1 breakfastcup flour
1 dessertspoonful sugar
1 egg (well beaten)
1 teaspoon Baking Powder
¾ breakfastcup milk
1 oz. butter

Mix flour, sugar, and Baking Powder together, then mix egg and milk, make a well in centre of dry ingredients, and mix to a smooth paste with milk. Cook in small lots on hot greased girdle.

SPONGE SANDWICH.

3 eggs
1 cup sugar (small)
1 cup flour (small)
½ teaspoon Baking Powder

Beat eggs and sugar well, then add flour and baking powder mixed; bake in hot oven in sandwich tins.

RENE'S KISSES.

½ lb. cornflour
½ lb. butter
½ lb. sugar
½ lb. flour
4 eggs
2 teaspoonfuls Baking Powder

Cream butter and sugar, add eggs beaten and flavouring, mix baking powder, flour, and cornflour, and add to mixture; mix until quite light, drop in teaspoon lots on cold oven shelf, bake in quick oven; when cold, fasten together with jam.

CHRISTMAS CAKE.

1 lb. butter
1 lb. currants
1 lb. raisins
1 lb. sultanas
¼ lb. mixed peel
¼ lb. almonds
4 breakfastcups flour
2 breakfastcups sugar
10 eggs
1 heaped teaspoon Baking Powder
Wine glass brandy

Beat butter to a cream, add sugar, then eggs one by one (unbeaten); mix baking powder with flour, and put in, then fruit dredged with flour. Brandy. Cook 4½ hours, moderate oven.

EXPRESS CAKES.

1 breakfastcup flour
1 teacup sugar
2 teaspoonfuls Baking Powder
3 eggs
¼ cup milk
(Essence vanilla or lemon)

Mix flour, sugar, and baking powder together, beat in the eggs and milk, put into small greased tins. Bake in moderate oven about 20 minutes.

NEW ZEALAND BUNS.

1 breakfastcup flour
1 tablespoonful sugar
1 heaped teaspoon Baking Powder
1 egg
3 ozs. butter

Rub the butter into flour, sugar, and baking powder, then add the egg well beaten, and enough milk to make a stiff dough. Place in heaps on cold greased oven shelf. Bake quick oven 10 to 15 minutes.

SPONGE CAKE.

2 level breakfastcups flour
1 level breakfastcup sugar
4 tablespoons milk
2 teaspoons Baking Powder
4 eggs
Pinch salt

Beat the eggs, then beat in the sugar, add salt and milk. Mix flour and powder together in dry state, then sift it in; beat all together, and bake in quick oven.

ROCK CAKES.

1 breakfastcup flour
2 heaped dessertspoonfuls sugar
2 ozs. currants
2 ozs. butter (or lard)
1 oz. or 1 round candied peel
1 dessertspoonful Baking Powder
Milk to mix

Rub the butter (or lard) into flour, then add other dry ingredients, the egg beaten, and sufficient milk to make stiff dough. Place in rocky shapes on cold greased oven shelf, and bake in hot oven 10 or 12 minutes.

CHILDREN'S CAKES.

2 breakfastcups flour
3 ozs. dripping
1 teaspoonful Baking Powder
¼ lb. sugar
¼ lb. sultanas
1 oz. peel
½ teaspoonful salt
1 egg

MODE.—Rub dripping well into the flour, add all dry ingredients. Beat the egg well, mix with a breakfastcup nearly full of milk. Mix all together, and bake in greased patty-tins about 15 minutes.

SHORTBREAD.

½ lb. flour (or one breakfastcup)
¼ lb. butter
2 ozs. sugar (or 2 tablespoonfuls)

Cream butter and sugar, then work in the flour, continue to work until it becomes a firm dough. Place into an ungreased tin, press well down with the knuckles, then smooth over with a knife, and prick with fork. Bake in a slow oven 1 hour. Cut into shapes whilst hot in the tin.

FRUIT CAKE.

2 breakfastcups flour
½ lb. butter
½ lb. sugar
1 teaspoon Baking Powder
8 eggs
1 teaspoon ground nutmeg
1 lb. currants
4 ozs. almonds
½ lb. mixed peel

MODE.—Beat butter to a cream, add sugar gradually, then white of eggs (beaten 10 minutes), then yolks (beaten 10 minutes), then flour and other ingredients. Bake 2½ hours moderate oven.

PANCAKES.

2 breakfastcups flour
2 teaspoonfuls Baking Powder
Pinch of salt

Mix well in dry state, add two eggs, well beaten, and enough milk to make thin batter. Fry with lard or butter.

SPONGE ROLL.

1 cup flour
1 tea cup sugar
3 eggs
1 teaspoon Baking Powder
2 tablespoons cold water

METHOD.—Beat eggs and sugar till stiff and frothy, sift flour and baking powder, add water to eggs and sugar, then stir in the sifted flour and baking powder lightly and quickly, pour into greased tin, and bake in hot oven from 8 to 10 minutes. This recipe will also serve for a Jam Sandwich.

RICE CAKES.

1 cup flour
½ cup ground rice
¼ lb. sugar
3 ozs. butter
1 egg
½ cup milk
1 teaspoonful Baking Powder
A pinch of salt

Cream butter and sugar, sift dry ingredients together, whisk the egg well, and mix all thoroughly. Add flavouring, and a few currants if liked. Bake in patty pans in moderate oven about 10 minutes.

SUNBEAM CAKE.

½ lb. sugar
½ lb. butter
½ lb. sultanas
¼ lb. peel
¾ lb. flour
6 eggs
1 small teaspoonful Baking Powder
A few almonds and flavouring

Mode.—Whip butter and sugar to a cream, beat in eggs one by one, then add flour and baking powder, fruit, peel, almonds, and flavouring. Bake in moderate oven 2 hours.

GRATED NUT CAKES.

1½ breakfastcups flour
¼ lb. desiccated coconut (or almonds)
6 tablespoonfuls sugar
4 ozs. butter
½ teacup milk
1 dessertspoonful Egg Powder

Mix coconut with the flour, sugar, and Egg Powder. Soften the butter a little, then rub it lightly into the other ingredients, moisten the whole with the milk slightly warmed, and bake in moderate quick oven in buttered patty pans.

AFTERNOON TEA CAKES.

1 breakfastcup flour
2 heaped dessertspoonfuls sugar
3 ozs. butter (or 3 tablespoonfuls)
1 egg (well beaten) and some milk
1 teaspoon Baking Powder
Jam (raspberry preferred)

Rub butter into flour, then add sugar and Baking Powder, mix well, add egg and sufficient milk to make a light dough. Roll and cut into rounds; place a little raspberry jam on each, wet the edges, and press them together. Put on cold, greased oven shelf, and bake about 10 minutes.

MADEIRA CAKE.

3 eggs, their weight in butter and sugar
The weight of 4 eggs in flour
1 teaspoonful Baking Powder
Juice of one small lemon

Cream butter and sugar, add eggs one by one, beat well, add lemon juice, flour, and baking powder. Bake in buttered cake tin in moderate oven for about one hour. Ice the top if desired.

RICE CAKES (Without Eggs).

1 cup flour
½ cup ground rice
¼ lb. sugar
4 ozs. butter
½ cup milk (good measure)
1 heaped teaspoonful Egg Powder
Pinch salt

Cream butter and sugar, sift and mix dry ingredients into same, mix all thoroughly with the milk, add flavouring, and bake in patty pans in moderate oven from 10 to 12 minutes.

WALNUT CAKE.

1 large cup flour
1 small cup sugar
1 small cup butter
1 tablespoon cocoa
1 teaspoon Baking Powder
1 cup walnuts
3 eggs

Beat butter and sugar to a cream, add eggs well beaten, mix cocoa with a little milk, then add the other ingredients, and bake in shallow cake tin in moderate oven. When cold, ice with water icing, and place some walnuts halved on top.

Currants should be rubbed in a colander with a little flour before using.

CHOCOLATE CAKES.

¼ lb. flour
¼ lb. sugar
2 eggs
2 tablespoonfuls butter
1 teaspoon chocolate (or 1½ teaspoons cocoa)
½ teaspoonful vanilla essence
½ teaspoonful Baking Powder

Beat butter and sugar together, then add flour, baking powder, cocoa and essence. Bake in moderate oven 15 to 20 minutes in sandwich tins. Ice with chocolate icing.

LEMON BISCUITS.

½ lb. butter
½ lb. sugar
1 lb. (or 2 breakfastcups) flour
2 eggs
1 teaspoonful Baking Powder
Flavour with essence of lemon

Cream butter and sugar together, add eggs, then flour and powder mixed well, roll out thin, cut into shapes and bake.

A GOOD PLAIN CAKE.

Mix well together two breakfastcups of flour, two teaspoonfuls Baking Powder, a little salt and spice, and ¼ lb. sugar. Rub in ½ lb. butter, then mix in 6 ozs. sultanas, 2 ozs. currants, a few pieces sliced peel. Beat 3 eggs and half-cupful milk together, and moisten the lot. Bake in quick oven thoroughly.

DATE CAKE.

½ lb. butter
½ lb. sugar
6 eggs
½ lb. dates
1½ breakfastcups flour
1 teaspoonful Baking Powder

Beat butter and sugar to a cream, add eggs 2 at a time; beat well, add flour, powder, and fruit. Bake about 1½ hours.

PYRAMIDS.

1 breakfastcup flour
2 teaspoonfuls Baking Powder
1 teaspoonful cornflour (or potato flour)
¼ lb. sugar
¼ lb. butter
4 eggs
Flavouring

Beat butter and sugar to a cream, well whisk the eggs, sift dry ingredients together, make a hole in centre of flour, in which put butter and eggs, mix thoroughly but lightly; add flavouring liked, and bake in small patty pans in hot oven for about 10 minutes.

PICNIC DAINTIES.

1½ breakfastcups flour
3 tablespoonfuls butter
2 tablespoonfuls sugar
1 dessertspoonful Egg Powder
Milk to mix

Rub butter into flour, then stir in sugar, egg powder and sufficient milk to make firm dough. Roll and cut into rounds, place one teaspoonful of raspberry jam in the centre; wet the edges and press them together. Place on cold greased oven shelf. Bake 12 minutes.

GIRDLE CAKES.

Rub into two breakfastcups flour 6 ozs. of butter, add 3 teaspoonfuls Baking Powder, and mix thoroughly. Mix into this ¼ lb. currants, pinch salt, a little nutmeg, and make into light dough with milk. Roll out, cut into rounds, bake 15 minutes on a girdle or in the oven. If required sweet, add tablespoonful sugar.

SEED CAKE.

½ lb. butter
½ lb. sugar
6 eggs
2 cups flour
1 teaspoonful Baking Powder
Caraway seed, lemon peel

Beat butter and sugar to a cream, then add the eggs, beating in one by one with the hand; lastly, add flour and baking powder, mixed together, with seeds and lemon peel as desired.

GINGER CAKE.

2 breakfastcups flour
1 teacup sugar
1 teaspoon baking soda
1 teaspoon Baking Powder
1 teacup golden syrup
1 teacup butter
1 teacup milk
2 eggs
2 dessertspoonfuls ground ginger
1 teaspoonful cinnamon
½ teaspoonful spice

Mix dry ingredients, add eggs well beaten, and butter (melted) last of all; bake three-quarters of an hour.

VICTORIA SANDWICH.

2 level breakfastcups flour
1 level breakfastcup sugar
4 ozs. butter
3 eggs
2 teaspoons Baking Powder
1 small cup water
Essence flavouring to taste

Warm the butter, and beat in the sugar, drop in the eggs one at a time, then the flour with the baking powder mixed, must be lightly beaten in; add flavouring and water gradually. The baking powder may be added last of all to give better results. Bake in quick oven 15 minutes.

SULTANA CAKE.

1 lb. flour
½ lb. butter
½ lb. sultanas
½ lb. sugar
4 eggs
3 ozs. peel
1 heaped teaspoonful Baking Powder
A little milk

Cream the butter and sugar together, add eggs well beaten, then the other ingredients; bake in moderate oven two hours

LEMON TEA CAKES.

Rub into 1½ breakfastcups of flour 3 tablespoonfuls each of lard and butter; add 6 ozs. moist sugar, the grated rind of one lemon, a little of the juice, and a heaped teaspoonful of Baking Powder. Mix into moderate paste, with 2 well beaten eggs. Divide into cakes; place on greased oven shelf, and bake in brisk oven 20 minutes.

TEA CAKES (Without Eggs).

1 lb. flour
4 ozs. sugar
4 ozs. butter
2 teaspoonfuls Egg Powder
½ lb. dates (or sultanas) chopped
Milk to mix, salt a pinch

Rub butter into flour, add all dry ingredients, mix all together to a paste with milk, turn out on board, form into a roll, and cut in equal parts, put on cold greased and floured tray, and bake in quick oven.

TENNIS BUNS.

1 breakfastcup flour
3 heaped dessertspoonfuls sugar
1 teaspoon Baking Powder
1 egg
3 ozs. butter
Candied peel and milk
Essence of lemon to taste

Rub butter into flour, add other dry ingredients, mix well, then add the egg well beaten, and enough milk to make a stiff dough. Place in small lots on a cold greased oven shelf. Put a piece of candied peel on top of each. Bake in quick oven about 10 minutes.

"EGG POWDER" ROCK CAKES.

1 breakfastcup flour
2 dessertspoonfuls sugar
2 ozs. currants
4 ozs. butter (or lard)
½ oz. or 1 round candied peel
1 dessertspoonful Egg Powder
Milk to mix

Rub the butter (or lard) into flour, add the other dry ingredients, and sufficient milk to make a stiff dough, place on cold greased oven shelf in rocky shapes. Bake in hot oven.

COFFEE CAKE.

¼ lb. butter (or dripping)
¼ lb. sugar
½ cup Golden Syrup
1 large cup of strong coffee
1 lb. flour (or 2 breakfastcups)
2 heaped teaspoonfuls Baking Powder
1 teaspoonful ground ginger
A few raisins and peel
A little spice or nutmeg

Cream butter and sugar, add syrup warmed and mixed with the coffee, together with sifted flour, add spices to creamed butter, add raisins and peel, then beat in baking powder; bake in moderate oven about 2 hours.

BATH BUNS.

½ cupful butter
1 cupful sugar
3 eggs
½ cupful lemon peel (cut up)
3 breakfastcups flour
3 teaspoons Baking Powder

Beat butter and sugar to a cream, add the eggs, and beat few minutes longer, add other ingredients, and mix into moderate paste with milk. Place on cold oven shelf (greased), and bake about 12 or 15 minutes in hot oven.

Special.—If Baking Powder should appear lumpy in tin, it will easily powder up again (with back of spoon) before using in cooking.

SMALL COCONUT CAKES.

1 breakfastcup flour
4 ozs. desiccated coconut
2 dessertspoonfuls sugar
1 teaspoon Baking Powder
2 ozs butter (or 2 tablespoonfuls)
Milk

Rub butter into flour, mix in coconut, baking powder, and sugar, making into stiff dough with milk. Place in small lots on cold greased oven shelf, and bake in hot oven about 20 minutes.

COCONUT DELICACIES.

½ breakfastcup flour (or ¼ lb.)
½ breakfastcup coconut (or ¼ lb.) desiccated
3 ozs. butter (or 3 tablespoonfuls)
2 heaped dessertspoonfuls sugar
1 egg
1 teaspoon Baking Powder

Rub butter into flour, add other dry ingredients, and mix, then add egg beaten, this should make stiff dough (if not add very little milk, as dough must be stiff). Place on cold greased oven shelf in small lots. Bake in hot oven from 10 to 12 minutes.

ABOUT CAKE MIXING.

Always cream together the butter and sugar in a basin, before commencing to add the eggs already beaten; this will add success to your cakes.

MISCELLANEOUS

DELICIOUS TRIFLE.

Cut up stale sponge cakes in dish, spread over with jam (raspberry preferred), then make a pint custard, (as per direction for Custard), and pour when cooked over the cakes. Let stand till cold, then spread whipped cream on top. This dish is improved by adding a little sherry or wine to the cut sponges.

EGG DRINK (Without Eggs).

Two large cups of milk; take sufficient to mix smooth 1 heaped teaspoon of Custard Powder. Place remainder in saucepan with 2 teaspoonfuls sugar; when it boils add mixture, stir and place immediately into glasses (grate nutmeg on top to taste).

LEMON SPONGE.

½ packet isinglass or gelatine
5 ozs. loaf sugar
¾ pint cold water
2 lemons
Whites of 2 eggs

Soak the isinglass or gelatine in ¾ pint cold water, then dissolve over the fire with the rind of two lemons thinly pared, add the sugar and the juice of 2 lemons. Boil all together 2 or 3 minutes; strain and let it remain until nearly cold, and beginning to set, then add the white of 2 eggs, well beaten, and whisk 10 minutes, when it will become the consistence of sponge; put it lightly into a glass dish immediately, leaving it in appearance as rocky as possible.

All fruit sponges are made in the same way. If syrups are used for flavouring, use ¾ oz. gelatine.

TO MAKE A CUSTARD.

From a pint of new milk take enough to mix smooth one large dessertspoonful of Custard Powder, sweeten the remainder of the milk to taste (say, a heaped dessertspoonful sugar), and when the milk is boiling, pour the mixed custard into it, stir and pour immediately into jug. When cold, place in glasses (grate nutmeg on if desired).

LEMON HONEY (For Sponges or Tarts).

1 lb. sugar
Rind and juice of 4 lemons
4 ozs. butter
4 eggs

Grate only the yellow part of the lemon rinds (avoid white part, as it is bitter), strain the juice, beat eggs a little, put all ingredients into enamelled pot; cook slowly until thick and smooth. Do not let it boil. Put in jar, and cover when cold.

PINEAPPLE JELLY.

1 tin pineapple chunks
2 packets White's jelly crystals

Cut up pineapple into small dice, dividing fruit and juice into two jelly moulds; make jellies separately, using little less water than directed, then pour into moulds.

FIG AND BANANA SALAD.

Slice in equal quantities some nice bananas and freshly preserved figs, sprinkle castor sugar over each layer, add lemon juice if desired, place in glass dish, and cover with whipped cream flavoured with vanilla, put in a cool place for 2 hours.

BAKED PEARS.

Pears
Golden syrup
Water

Wipe some large sound pears, arrange them in an enamel baking dish with stalk ends upwards, pour a little water over them, and enough golden syrup to sweeten (say one tablespoonful to every three pears). Bake in a slow oven 2 hours or more. If baked slowly they will be juicy, tender and sweet, baste them frequently with the syrup and water, if oven is too hot cover with oven shelf. Serve with cream or custard.

TOMATO AND MACARONI.

¼ lb. macaroni
Tomatoes, onion, butter
Pepper and salt

Break up macaroni and boil in plenty of water slightly salted, boil one onion in the same water, strain and put a layer in a buttered pie dish, put next a layer of sliced tomato and the boiled onion, another layer of macaroni, and so on with pepper and salt on each layer till dish is full; have tomato on top layer, sprinkle bread crumbs over, and some little pieces of butter. Bake till tomatoes are cooked about one hour.

PEAR GINGER.

6 lb. pears (nearly ripe)
1 lb. preserved ginger (full lb.)
4 lbs. sugar

Cut up pears, and let stand over night with sugar on, boil with ginger following day until soft.

TOMATO SAUCE (No. 1).

12 lbs. tomatoes
2 lbs. onions
2 ozs. garlic (chopped fine)
1 oz. ground ginger
½ oz. cloves
4 ozs. salt
½ oz. cayenne pepper

Place spices in a bag, and boil with rest of ingredients 2 hours (occasionally squeeze the spice bag), then beat through a sieve or colander till nothing but skin and seed remains. When cool, add a quart of best malt vinegar, half a lb. brown sugar, boil again until it is as thick as cream. Bottle and cork when cold. Always put sauce in small bottles if convenient, it keeps better, and seal top of same.

TOMATO SAUCE (No. 2).

12 lbs. tomatoes
2 lb. cooking apples
1 lb. onions
¾ lb. sugar
¼ lb. salt
2 ozs. each of allspice and garlic
¼ oz. each of chillies, mace and cloves
1 quart best English malt vinegar

Wipe and break the tomatoes, cut up garlic, apples, and onions. Boil all together with rest of ingredients 3 to 4 hours. Strain and bottle.

TOMATO SOUP.

2 lbs. tomatoes
1 oz. butter
2 ozs. sago
1 large onion
1 quart stock
Pepper and salt

Slice the tomatoes and onion, and boil in stock until tender, strain through a colander, and return to the saucepan, then add butter, sago, and seasoning; boil till sago is cooked.

APPLE SAUCE.

Pare and core six large apples, cut up, and stew half hour with small cup of water, then add small cup sugar, mash together with a wooden stirrer.

EASY BREAKFAST OR TEA DISH.

Stew gently some tomatoes with a little butter, pepper and salt, when soft mash with a fork, and add to them a well-beaten egg until they thicken. Serve on hot buttered toast.

WHITE SAUCE.

Boil 1 pint of rich milk. Stir into it 1 tablespoonful of flour, previously made smooth in a little milk. To this add salt (and, if preferred, 1 teaspoonful of olive oil). Serve hot. For parsley sauce, just add before serving half teaspoonful of finely-chopped parsley.

APPLE CHUTNEY.

4 lbs. green apples
2 lbs. onions
2 lbs. brown sugar
½ lb. raisins
2 teaspoonfuls salt
1 teaspoonful cayenne pepper
1 teaspoonful ground cloves
1 oz. garlic

Chop ingredients up fine (or put all through a mincer, except apples, salt, pepper, and cloves). Cut apples as for stewing, put all into pot, cover with vinegar, boil slowly 4 or 5 hours.

TOMATO SAUSAGE.

2 lbs. mutton, fat and lean (or any cold meat)
1 lb. tomatoes
¾ oz. black pepper
1 oz. salt, and little grated nutmeg

Put meat through fine mincer, mash the tomatoes, and rub through a sieve, removing skins. Mix meat and tomatoes together, add beaten egg to bind, form into cakes, roll in flour, egg, and bread crumbs, and fry in boiling fat.

SALAD DRESSING.

½ teaspoonful mustard
Pinch of salt
Little pepper
2 heaped dessertspoonfuls sugar
Yolks of 2 hard-boiled eggs

Mix all together, add sufficient milk (breakfastcup), then vinegar, stirring it until it thickens.

SAVOURY OMELETTE.

4 eggs
1 tablespoon flour
Large breakfastcup milk
Parsley, onion, salt and pepper to taste

Beat eggs, mix flour smooth with a little of the milk, then add remainder; stir into the eggs, add parsley, onion, pepper and salt; put a small piece of butter or dripping in frying-pan, pour in the mixture, and cook gradually. When brown underneath, cut in pieces, and turn.

VEGETARIAN ROAST.

Bread
Peanuts
Milk, seasoning
1 onion

Brown some crusts of bread in the oven, shell peanuts and put them through the mincer, putting the bread through the mincer afterwards.

Take a cup of the bread crumbs, pour on them a little milk, just enough to moisten, but not to make them too soft.

Mix with them half a cup of the ground peanuts, salt, and a little powdered herb, either sage or thyme, and one minced onion, put all into a buttered pie dish, and bake slowly till nicely browned. If it appears to be getting too dry, a very little water may be put on top as it is cooking, or a few pieces of butter on top makes a fine improvement.

HAM OR TONGUE OMELETTE.

Is made by adding about 2 tablespoonfuls of grated ham or tongue to the egg mixture, before it is cooked, omitting parsley.

Ambrosial Jam

8 peaches, peeled
3 large oranges
1 pulp of 1 med. cantaloupe
1 lemon
1 (8 1/2 oz.) can crushed
1 pineapple
1 sugar

Chop all ingredients fine. Put oranges through food chopper. Combine all with 3/4 cup sugar for every 1 cup of fruit. Mix well and let stand overnight.

Next morning, gently cook mixture 1 hour, stirring frequently. Pour into hot jars and seal. Makes 8 pints.

Apple Maple Jam

3 quart finely chopped apples (about 6 pound; ds) 6 cup sugar
1 cup maple syrup
1 teaspoon cinnamon
1/2 teaspoon allspice
1/2 teaspoon nutmeg
1/4 teaspoon cloves

Combine all ingredients in a large sauce pot. Bring slowly to a boil. Cook rapidly to jellying point. As mixture thickens, stir frequently to prevent sticking. Pour hot into hot jars, leaving ¼ inch head space. Adjust caps. Process 10 minutes in boiling water bath. Yield: about 8 half pints.

Fresh Strawberry Jam

6 cup strawberries -- sliced
2 boxes pectin
1 3/4 cup honey
2 tablespoon lemon juice

In saucepan, combine strawberries and pectin, mashing or crushing berries to blend completely. Bring mixture to a boil. Boil hard for one minute, stirring constantly. Add honey and lemon juice. Return to a rolling boil for five minutes, stirring constantly. Remove from heat. Skim off foam. Ladle into hot sterilized jars. Seal. Makes eight 1/2 pints.

Cranberry Preserve

2 medium apples
3 cup sugar
3/4 cup water
4 1/2 cup cranberries
1 tablespoon grated lemon peel
1/4 cup creme de cassis

Peel, core and coarsely dice apples. Heat sugar and water in heavy large saucepan over low heat, swirling pan occasionally, until sugar dissolves. Add cranberries, apples and lemon peel. Bring to boil.

Reduce heat to medium and cook until consistency of thick jam, stirring frequently, about 20 minutes. Stir in cassis to taste. Cool completely before serving. (Can be stored in refrigerator 1 month.)

Cranberry-Orange Jam

4 cup (1 lb) fresh or frozen cranberries 3 cup water
3/4 cup orange juice
1/4 cup lemon juice
4 cup sugar
2 pouches certo liquid pectin

Place cranberries and water in a heavy-bottomed 8-10 qt pan. Bring to a boil over high heat; reduce heat and simmer, uncovered, until berries begin to pop (about 10 minutes). Drain well, reserving liquid. Place cranberries in a blender or food processor and whirl until smooth; add enough of the reserved liquid to berries to make 4 cups.

Return berry puree to pan. Stir in orange juice, lemon juice, and sugar until well blended. Bring to a full rolling boil over high heat, stirring constantly; then boil, stirring for one minute. Remove from heat and stir in pectin all at once. Skim off any foam.

Ladle hot jam into hot, sterilized half-pint jars, leaving 1/4"
head space. Wipe rims and threads clean, seal, etc.
Process for 5 minutes in boiling water bath. Makes about 6 half pints.

Instant Raspberry Cordial Jam

12 oz raspberry jam
1 tablespoon to 2 chambord or other
1 raspberry liqueur

Stir liqueur into jam; cover and refrigerate at least one day to allow flavors to meld.

Cranberry-Raspberry Preserve

6 cup raspberries (3 pints)
2 1/2 cup sugar
3 cup cranberries (12 oz. bag)
1/4 cup fresh orange juice
1 grated zest of 1 orange

Stir together the raspberries and 1 cup of the sugar in a medium bowl and let stand for 1 hour. Stir the cranberries and the remaining sugar together in a nonreactive shallow preserving pan and place over high heat. Stir constantly so the sugar does not burn until the cranberries begin to release juice, about 5 minutes. Continue cooking until al the cranberries have popped and the mixture is syrupy and comes to a boil. Skim off any foam that forms on top and continue to cook and stir until the mixture thickens, about 10 minutes more. Add the raspberries and all their juice and cook for 10 minutes more.

Stir in the orange juice and zest. Remove a small amount of the jam to a saucer and place in the freezer for 5 minutes. If the mixture wrinkles when pushed to one side, it is ready. If not, continue cooking for 5 minutes and retest. When the preserves are the right consistency, turn down the heat to a simmer and ladle into hot sterilized jars. Wipe the rims clean with a damp towel and seal with new lids and metal rings. Process in a hot-water bath for 5 minutes.

Remove, cook, check seals, label, and store. Makes 4 one pint jars.

Rose Petal Jam

30 large red cabbage roses
3 lb sugar
2 pint water
1/2 lemon

Take the roses and cut off the white ends. Make a syrup with the sugar and water. Then add the juice of the half a lemon and the rose petals. Boil until the roses crystal ize, stirring frequently with a wooden spoon. Turkish cooks keep this for years.

Dried Fig Jam

28 oz dried figs
5 cup ; water
1/2 cup fresh lemon juice
3 cup sugar
1 seeds from juiced lemons
1 teaspoon ground cardamom
1 tablespoon dark rum

Place figs in 4 qt pot. Add all water, cover pot, bring to a boil and remove pot from heat. Let the pot of figs sit for at least an hour to plump them. Remove figs from the dark water with a slotted spoon.

Reserve the water. Cut stems off figs with scissors and chop figs medium coarse by hand or in a processor. Add lemon juice and sugar to the fig water. Set water to a second boil, then reduce heat and let simmer for 5-10 minutes. Tie up seeds into a cheesecloth bundle and drop in fig water. Drop the chopped figs into the fig water. Bring fig jam to another boil, then let simmer for 15-20 minutes. Jam should be slightly thickened. Remove from heat. Take out the cheesecloth bag. Stir in the rum and cardamom well. Ladle into 1 pint jars (1/2 pint works, too), leaving 1/4" head space. Seal jars according to manufacturer's instructions. Process jars for 15 minutes in a boiling water bath. Yield: About 4 pints.

Sweet Onion Jam

6 medium sweet onions, sliced
4 tablespoon butter
2 teaspoon vegetable oil
1/2 teaspoon salt
1/3 cup brown sugar

In heavy skillet, melt butter and vegetable oil. Add onions and saute until they are slightly brown. Season with salt. Reduce heat, stirring constantly until caramel color and tender. Stir in brown sugar until dissolved. Put in jars and refrigerate until ready to serve. May be heated again. Serve with chicken or turkey.

Apricot~ Orange and Almond Jam

1 lb dried apricots
2 oz split almonds
3 oranges
2 lemons
2 1/2 lb sugar
2 1/2 teaspoon ground cinnamon

Chop the apricots roughly. Put them into a large bowl, sprinkling the fine grated zest of the oranges and the cinnamon between layers.

Squeeze the juice of the oranges, measure and add enough water to make 3 pints in all. Pour the liquids over the fruit; leave to soak overnight in a cool place.

Ginger Peach Jam

4 1/2 cup prepared fruit (about 3 1/4 lbs fullly ripe peaches)
1/4 cup finely chopped crystallized ginger
6 cup sugar
1 box sure-jell fruit pectin

Peel and pit peaches; finely chop or grind.
Measure 4 1/2 cups into 6-to 8-quart saucepot; add ginger.
Measure sugar and set aside. Mix fruit pectin into fruit in saucepot.
Place over high heat and stir until mixture comes to a full boil.
Immediately add all sugar and stir. B ring to a full rolling boil and boil 1 minute, stirring constantly. Remove from heat and skim off foam with metal spoon. Ladle quickly into hot jars, filling within 1/8 inch of tops. Wipe jar rims and threads. Cover with two-piece lids. Screw bands tightly. Invert jars for 5 minutes, then turn upright. After 1 hour, check seals.*
*Or follow water bath method recommended by USDA.
Makes about 8 (1 cup) jars

Ground Cherry Jam

2 lb ground cherries; husked
4 cup sugar
1 cup water
2 lemons; grated rind and juice
Husk and wash the ground cherries carefully. Measure the sugar and water into a large kettle. Bring to a full rolling boil, and boil for 2 minutes.

Add the cherries, lemon rinds, and juice. Bring to a full rolling boil again, reduce heat and simmer for 5 minutes. Remove from heat, cover with a clean towel, and let stand overnight.

Next day, return to the heat, and again bring to boil. Reduce heat and cook gently until transparent (about 15 minutes). Immediately pour into hot, sterilized glasses seal at once. Yields 5 to 6 cups.

Grandma Howard's Tomato Jam

1/2 orange
1/2 lemon
3 cup tomatoes; peeled, chopped about 1 3
1 pkg pectin crystals; 57 g
4 1/2 cup sugar, granulated

Halve and seed orange and lemon. In food processor, finely shop fruit with rind. Transfer to heavy saucepan; add tomatoes and bring to a boil. Reduce heat and simmer for 10 minutes or until rind is tender.

Stir in pectin. Return to boil; boil for 1 minute, stirring. Stir in sugar; bring to a full rolling boil. Boil, stirring, for 1 minute.

Remove from heat and skim off foam. Pour into hot sterilized jars, leaving 1/4 inch head space. Seal jars; process in boiling water bath for 10 minutes. Store in cool, dark, dry place. MAKES: ABOUT 5 CUPS

Island Jam

4 cup cantaloupe, peeled and
1 diced
3 oranges, peeled and diced
1/4 cup lemon juice
4 cup sugar
1 teaspoon lemon rind
1 teaspoon orange rind
1/2 teaspoon salt
3 cup bananas

Combine cantaloupe, oranges, and 1/4 cup lemon juice in heavy saucepan. Bring to a boil and simmer for 15 minutes. Add sugar, lemon rind, orange rind, and salt. Continue simmering for 30 minutes. Add 3 cups sliced bananas and continue simmering for an additional 15minutes. Pour into jelly jars and cover with paraffin. Can be frozen. Yield 8 (6 ounce) jars

Fat-Free Jam Granola

10 cup rolled oats
1 teaspoon salt
1 teaspoon vanilla
1/4 cup honey
1 10-oz jar (apricot or any 1 flavor) jam
Mix together thoroughly in a large bowl, using your hands. Spread this mixture out on a large cookie sheet, and bake at 350 for about a half hour until it's starting to brown, taking it out every five minutes or so to stir it around.

Pear-Apple Jam

2 cup finely chopped pears (peeled and core; d) 1 cup finely chopped apples
(peeled and cor; ed) 6 1/2 cup sugar
1/4 teaspoon ground cinnamon
1/3 cup bottled lemon juice
6 oz liquid pectin
Yield: About 7 to 8 half-pints

Procedure: Crush apples and pears in a large saucepan and stir in cinnamon.
Thoroughly mix sugar and lemon juice with fruits and bring to a boil over high
heat, stirring constantly. Immediately stir in pectin. Bring to a full rolling boil and
boil hard 1 minute, stirring constantly. Remove from heat, quickly skim off foam,
and fill sterile jars leaving 1/4-inch head space.

Adjust lids and process as recommended in Table 1.

Table 1. Recommended process time for Pear-Apple Jam in a boiling water
canner.
Style of Pack: Hot. Jar Size: Half-Pints. Process Time at Altitudes of 0 - 1,000 ft: 5
min.
1,001 - 6,000 ft: 10 min.
Above 6,000 ft: 15 min.

Lebanon County Rhubarb Jam

2 1/2 lb rhubarb
1/2 cup water
1 1/2 lb sugar
Rind and juice of 2 oranges

Wash and skin the rhubarb and cut into small pieces; add sugar and 1/2 cup of
cold water. Grate the rind of the oranges and add to the rhubarb. Add the orange
juice and cook for 30 minutes, stirring occasionally. Pour into sterilized jars and
seal.

Pineapple-Apricot Jam

20 oz pineapple; crushed, 1 cn
6 oz maraschino cherries; 1 jar,*
8 oz dried apricots; cut into 1/4
1/4 cup water
3 1/2 cup sugar
2 tablespoon lemon juice
3 oz fruit pectin; liquid,1 pouch

* Drain, reserving 1/3 cup of the syrup, the cherries and cut up in smal pieces. Heat the pineapple, with the syrup, the reserved cherry syrup, the apricots and the water to boiling in a Dutch oven, stirring occasionally then reduce the heat and cover. Simmer, stirring occasionally, until the apricots are tender, about 10 minutes. Stir in the sugar, lemon juice, and cherries. Heat to a full rolling boil over high heat, stirring constantly. Boil and stir for 1 minute.

Remove from the heat and stir in the pectin. Pour into hot sterilized jars or glasses or freezer containers. Cover and cool to room temperature and store in the refrigerator or freezer no more than 3 months.

Apricot, Orange and Almond Jam

1 lb dried apricots
2 oz split almonds
3 oranges
2 lemons
2 1/2 lb sugar
2 1/2 teaspoon ground cinnamon

Chop the apricots roughly. Put them into a large bowl, sprinkling the fine grated zest of the oranges and the cinnamon between layers. Squeeze the juice of the oranges, measure and add enough water to make 3 pints in all. Pour the liquids over the fruit and leave to soak overnight in a cool place.

Quick Spiced Peach Jam

2 tablespoon water
2 tablespoon lemon juice
1/4 teaspoon cloves
1/2 teaspoon cinnamon
4 cup cut-up peaches
3 cup sugar

Combine the water, lemon juice, cloves and cinnamon in a quart saucepan. Dip the peaches in boiling water for 30 seconds and rinse in cold water. Peel and cut in small pieces into a measuring cup. Add them a cup full at a time to the saucepan, giving them a quick stir. When al the peaches are in the saucepan, bring to a boil and cook until soft, stirring frequently. This should take 6-8 minutes.

Stirring with one hand, add the sugar with the other. Stir over moderate heat until he mixture boils. Increase the heat and cook until the mixture thickens or measure 220 degrees F on the thermometer.

Pour into hot, clean jars, leaving 1/4 inch head space. Wipe the rims and put on the lids and screw bands very firmly, then process in a boiling water bath for 10 minutes. Cool, label and store in a dark place.

Fig Jam With Honey

1 cup honey equals 1 cup sugar. Peel figs, measure and add 3/4 cup honey for each cup fruit and let cook slowly, stirring constantly.

When thick, pour into jars to within 1/4 inch of top. Put on cap, screw band firmly tight. Process in boiling water bath 10 minutes. A little sliced lemon or chopped walnuts in fig jam makes it delicious.

Rose Hip Jam

4 quart rose hips with black ends
1 removed
1 (about 5 pounds)
3 1/2 cup sugar
1 x water (wine or sherry)

Gather the rose hips after the first frost. I am not sure why this is done but I have several sources that say to do it, including my grandmother, so I wait. Wash the rose hips well in case there is any insecticide residue. Cover with water and simmer until the hips are very soft and falling apart. Press through a food mill or colander to remove the seeds and larger particles. Press through a finer sieve to remove the smal er fibers and seed bits.
Cook the pulp down until it is quite thick. How thick? That is hard to say. Thicker than heavy cream. I check the measurements at this point. I add about a pound of sugar for every pound of pulp. The three 1/2 cups is my measurement from the last time I made this.

Add the sugar and check the taste. Sometimes I add a bit more sugar.

Rose hips have enough pectin to jel and enough ascorbic acid to make it a little tart. Cook over high heat until the mixture has a thick jam-like consistency. Put in jars. Makes 4 half-pint jars

Blueberry Jam

1/2 of a 6 oz can frozen apple; juice concentrate thawed 1 envelope plain gelatin
5 cup blueberries; fresh or frozen
1 tablespoon lemon juice
1/2 teaspoon ground nutmeg
1/8 teaspoon ground cinnamon

Pour the apple juice concentrate into a saucepan;sprinkle with gelatin and allow to soften for several minutes. Meanwhile,in a blender or a food processor finely chop blueberries. 1 cup at a time. Add lemon juice,spices, and 2 cups of chopped berries to gelatin; heat over medium-low until gelatin is dissolved. Remove from the heat; stir in remaining berries and mix well. Pour into jars or plastic containers; store in the refrigerator up to 3 weeks. Yield: 4 cups

Pear and Ginger Jam

2 lb pears
4 oz (1/2 cup) preserved ginger
2 lb (5 1/3 cups) sugar
1 1/4 cup water
1 oz (1) fresh ginger
1 juice of 2 lemons
Makes 2 lbs

Peel, core and dice the pears. Cut the preserved ginger into small chunks. Put all the ingredients into a preserving kettle and stir over a gentle heat until the sugar has dissolved. Bring to a boil and boil rapidly for about t 10 minutes, stirring occasionally, or until setting point is reached. Remove the piece of fresh ginger, lift out the fruit with a slotted spoon and place in hot clean jars.
Rapidly boil the syrup to reduce for a few minute s, then pour over the fruit to cover. Cover and process, then complete seals and cool.

Slide the contents of the bowl into a preserving pan and simmer gently until the fruit is beautifully tender. Check the fruit occasionally as it cooks and crush it down into the pan with a potato masher. It may need 1-1/4 hours to become really soft.
Warm the sugar. Add it to the pan together with the juice of the lemons and the almonds. Cook gently until the sugar is melted, then fast-boil until the saucer test shows that the preserve will set. Pot, tie down and label the preserve in the usual way. Makes enough to fill 5 jars.

Oriental Rhubarb Jam

1 lb rhubarb finely chopped
3 cup granulated sugar
1/2 teaspoon five spice powder
1/4 cup chopped candied ginger
1 x dash hot pepper sauce
3 tablespoon lemon juice

In a saucepan, combine rhubarb, sugar, five spice powder, ginger, hot pepper sauce and lemon juice; blend wel . Place over low heat, stirring constantly until sugar dissolves. Bring to boil, skim off foam and cook over medium heat, stirring frequently, until mixture becomes transparent and thickens, about 15 to 20 minutes. Ladle into hot, sterilized jars; seal. Makes about four 6 ounce jars.

Rhubarb, Rose, and Strawberry Jam

2 lb rhubarb, trimmed weight
1 lb small strawberries - slightly under; ripe 1/2 lb highly scented rose petals
1 1/2 lb sugar
4 small juicy lemons

Rhubarb is an unreliable setter so the inclusion of lemon juice in this recipe is essential and I like to play it safe by cooking the lemon pips with the fruit in order to extract their pectin. Slice the rhubarb and layer it in a large bowl with the whole hul ed strawberries and the sugar.

Pour on the lemon juice, cover and leave overnight.

Tip the contents of the bowl into a preserving pan. Add the lemon pips tied in a muslin bag and bring gently to a boil. Boil for 2 minutes then tip the contents of the pan back into the bowl. Cover and leave in a cool place over night once more. Put the rhubarb and strawberry mixture back into the pan. Pinch out the white tips from the bases of the rose petals and add the petals to the pan,pushing them well down among the fruit. Bring to the boil and fast boil until setting point is reached, then pot in warm sterilised jars in the usual way. Makes enough to fill 6 or 7 jars.

Sambuca Romana Jam

5 cup crushed, fresh blueberries
1/2 cup water
2 1/2 cup sugar
10 each coffee beans per jar
1 teaspoon grated lemon rind
1/2 cup sambuca romana
1 each box light fruit pectin

Mix 3/4 c sugar and pectin together. Stir into blueberries, lemon rind, water, and Sambuca in a heavy saucepan. Cook over high heat, stirring constantly, until mixture comes to a hard boil. Stir in remaining sugar.

Bring to a rolling boil, still stirring constantly. Boil for 1 minute.

Remove from heat. Skim off foam with metal spoon. Place 10 coffee beans in each jar. Immediately pour jam into hot sterilized jars and vacuum seal.
Makes 5 1/2 pint jars.

Apricot-Date Jam

1 cup dried apricots
1 cup unsweetened pineapple juice
1 cup pitted dates
1 teaspoon lemon juice
Soak apricots in pineapple juice overnight Blenderize all ingredients Serve as is on toast or thin with more pineapple juice to make a softer spread for waffles or pancakes Makes about 3 cups

Strawberry Jam

3 cup crushed strawberries
5 cup white sugar
1 pkg certo crystals
1 cup water

Mix together fruit and sugar and let stand for one hour. Boil water and certo crystals hard one minute. Add fruit and place in jars. Refrigerate.

Slide the contents of the bowl into a preserving pan and simmer gently until the fruit is beautifully tender. Check the fruit occasionally as it cooks and crush it down into the pan with a potato masher. It may need 1 1/4 hours to become really soft.

Warm the sugar. Add it to the pan together with the juice of the lemons and the almonds. Cook gently until sugar is melted, then fast-boil until the saucer test shows that the preserve will set. Pot, tie down and label the preserve in the usual way.

Concord Grape Jam

4 lb ripe concord grapes
1 cup water
7 1/2 cup sugar
1/4 cup powdered pectin

Squeeze the pulp from the grape skins into a preserving kettle, reserving the skins. Add the water to the kettle and simmer, covered, for 5 minutes. Strain the pulp to remove the seeds and return to the kettle. Grind the reserved skins and add them to the strained pulp. Stir in the sugar and pectin and bring slowly to a full rolling boil. Boil hard for 1 minute, stirring constantly.

Remove from heat and stir and skim for 5 minutes. Ladle into hot, sterilized jars and seal immediately.

Apricot-Raisin Jam

1/2 lb dried apricot halves, coarsely chopped 1 cup golden raisins
1 juice and grated rind of 1 lemon
1 cup orange juice
2 cup sugar

1. Place the apricots and raisins in a bowl and add water to cover.
Cover the bowl tightly and let it stand overnight. Drain the liquid into a large, heavy saucepan and chop the apricots coarsely. Add the apricots, raisins, lemon juice and rind, and orange juice to the pan, place over low heat, and bring to a simmer. Cook 20 minutes, stirring occasionally.

2. Add the sugar and continue cooking, stirring frequently until the mixture of fruit is very soft and the syrup sheets when dropped from the side of a spoon (220 degrees on a candy thermometer), 15 to 20 minutes. Spoon the jam into sterilized half-pint jars. Seal the jars, process in a boiling-water bath for 10 minutes and cool. Store in a cool, dark place.

Fig Preserve

6 quart figs
6 quart boiling water
8 cup sugar
3 quart water

POUR boiling water over figs. Let stand 15 minutes. Drain. Rinse figs in cold water. Prepare syrup by mixing sugar and water. Boil rapidly 10 minutes and skim, then drop figs into syrup a few at a time. Cook rapidly until figs are transparent. Lift out and place them in shallow pans. Boil syrup down until thick, pour over figs and let stand 6-8 hours. Sliced lemon or sliced preserved ginger may be added during 10 minute boiling. Fill sterilized jars to within ½ inch of top. Put on cap, screw bank FIRMLY TIGHT. Process in Boiling Water Bath 10 minutes or seal with paraffin.

Cooked Strawberry Jam - Certo Liquid

3 3/4 cup crushed fruit (2 qt)
1/4 cup lemon juice
7 cup sugar
1 pkg certo liquid *
YIELD 7 1/2 CUPS

* NOTE pk means 1 pouch containing 85 ml. ** A food processor may be used.
1. Wash jars and lids in hot soapy water, rinse and sterilize jars and lids by (1) boiling in water for 15 minutes (leave in water til needed.) Lids may be sterilized by placing in boiling water and boiling 5 minutes(leave in warm water til needed.) Utensils should also be sterilized.

2. Stem and crush well, one layer at a time, fully ripe berries.
Seive half of pulp to remove seeds if desired.

3. Using a liquid measuring cup, measure the exact amount of prepared fruit required and add to a large 4 to 8 qt pan. The pan should be no more than half full to allow mixture to reach a ful rolling boil.
Add lemon juice if required. 1/8 tsp butter may be added to reduce foaming.

4. Measure sugar. DO NOT REDUCE SUGAR. Add the exact amount of sugar specified and mix well.

5. Place pan over high heat; bring to a ful rolling boil and boil hard for 1 minute, stirring constantly. Remove from heat.

6. At once stir in Certo liquid.

7. Skim off foam with a metal spoon. Stir and skim for 5 minutes.

8. Pour quickly into prepared jars leaving 1/4 inch head room.

9. Seal jam at once with 2 piece metal lids or paraffin wax.

NOTE: Recipes using fruits with seeds 1/2 the fruit may be put through a seive, if desired.

Dutch Apple Pie Jam

1 lb tart green apples
1/2 cup raisins
1 cup water
1/3 cup lemon juice
1 teaspoon ground cinnamon
1/4 teaspoon ground allspice
4 1/2 cup granulated sugar
1 cup firmly packed light brown sugar 1/2 teaspoon margarine or butter
1 pouch certo liquid fruit pectin

Peel, core and finely chop enough apples to measure 2c Place in preserving kettle or Dutch oven with raisins,water, lemon juice,cinnamon and allspice. Stir in sugars and margarine/butter.

Place kettle over high heat and sitr until it comes to a full boil.

Boil hard for 1 minute, stirring constantly. Remove from heat and immediately stir in liquid fruit pectin. Bring to full rolling boil and boil hard for one minute, stirring constantly. Remove from heat.

Stir and skim foam for 5 minutes to prevent floating fruit. Pour quickly into sterilized jars, filling up to 1/2 in from the rim. Seal while hot with sterilized two-piece lids with new centres.

Fig-Strawberry Jam

3 1/2 cup mashed fresh figs (unpeeled) 3 cup sugar
1/4 cup lemon juice (optional)
3 pkg strawberry gelatin (3 ounces each)

Cook figs, sugar and lemon juice 5 to 7 minutes. Let stand overnight. Stir in gelatin. Boil again 3 to 4 minutes, stirring occasionally. Pour quickly into jars and seal at once, or store in refrigerator if used within a month.

Garlic Jam

4 garlic head, whole (~14 oz)
1 tablespoon olive oil, extra-virgin
1 medium onion; unpeeled and halved lengthwise 1 salt (opt)

Preheat the oven to 350F. Using a large sharp knife, cut off 1/2-inch from the top of each head of garlic to expose some of the flesh.

Drizzle 1 tablespoon of the oil over the bottom of a gratin or glass pie dish. Place the garlic and the onion halves cut sides down in the dish, cover tightly with foil and bake for 45 minutes, until very soft to the touch. Uncover and let cool for 20 minutes.

Peel the onion halves and finely chop them. Place in a medium bowl.

Squeeze the garlic pulp from the skins into the bowl; discard the skins. Using a fork, stir in the remaining 2 teaspoons oil and mash with the onion and garlic until thoroughly incorporated. Season with salt if desired. (The garlic jam will keep refrigerated in a glass jar for up to 2 weeks.) Makes 1-1/3 cups.

Use this condiment with roasted meats or as a spread for toasted croutons or cold meat sandwiches, or try a spoonful of it mixed into homemade salad dressings and sauces.

Apricot Jam

3 1/4 cup prepared fruit
1/2 bottle fruit pectin
7 cup sugar

Wash apricots. Pit. Do not peel. Cut in small pieces. Crush thoroughly. Combine sugar and fruit. Mix wel . Hat rapidly to full rolling boil. Stir constantly before and while boiling. Boil hard 1 minute. Remove from fire. Stir in fruit pectin. Skim.

Grape Jam

4 lb grapes
2 oranges; juiced and zested
5 cup sugar
1 cup raisins
1 pinch salt

Wash grapes and remove stems. Peel off skins and reserve; place grape pulp in a saucepan. Cook pulp over low heat 6 to 7 minutes, then press through a coarse sieve to remove seeds. Discard seeds; return pulp to saucepan. Add orange rind and juice, sugar, raisins and salt, and continue to cook over low heat, stirring constantly. As the mixture thickens, add grape skins and cook 6 to 8 minutes or until quite thick.

Pour into sterile hot jars and seal while hot.

Makes about 3 1/2 pints.

Greek Sour Cherry Preserve

1 lb black cherries
2 cup sugar
1/2 cup water
1 juice of half a lemon.

Pit cherries and place pits in a separate bowl. Layer cherries in saucepan with sugar. add water to the pits. Stir and drain and use this water to add to the cherries in saucepan. Let mixture stand for 1 hour. Then boil gently for 30 minutes, until syrup thickens. You may stir gently while cooking and skim off any scum that rises to the top. add the lemon juice at the end of the 30 minutes. Cool and store covered refrigerated.

Banana Jam

5 each ripe bananas
3 tablespoon fresh lime juice
2/3 cup fresh orange juice or water
1 1/2 cup sugar
1/2 vanilla bean split in half
1 lengthwise and cut into 1/3s
1/8 teaspoon salt
1 tablespoon banana liqueur (optional)

Peel the bananas and thinly slice or mash with a fork. Place the bananas in a heavy saucepan with the lime juice, orange juice, sugar, vanilla bean and salt, and bring to a boil. Reduce the heat and gently simmer the banana jam until htick, about 30 minutes, stirring often. Stir in the banana liqueur and remove the pan from the heat. Leave the vanilla bean in the jam - it's pretty.!

Spoon the jam into three 6-ounce canning jars that have been sterilized. Fill the jars to with-in one-eighth inch of the top.

Screw on the lids. Invert the jars for 5 minutes, then reinvert. Let the jam cool to room temperature.

Store the jam in a cool, dark place. Refrigerate the jam once opened; it will keep for several weeks.

Blackberry Jam

3 cup blackberries
2 cup water
1 pkg powdered fruit pectin
5 cup sugar

Crush fruit thoroughly. Add water and fruit pectin. Stir until pectin is dissolved. Heat to boiling. Boil 5-10 minutes. Add sugar. Stir until dissolved. Boil 3-5 minutes, stirring frequently, or until thick.

Berry Christmas Jam

3 cup fresh cranberries
1 medium seedless orange, peeled and quartered
1 pkg (10 oz) frozen sliced strawberries, slightly thawed
1/4 teaspoon ground cloves
1/4 teaspoon ground cinnamon
4 cup sugar
1/2 cup water
1 pouch (3 oz) liquid fruit pectin

In a food processor, combine the cranberries and orange quarters; process until coarsely chopped. Add strawberries, cloves and cinnamon; process until mixture is finely chopped. In a heavy large saucepan, combine fruit mixture, sugar and water until well blended.

Stirring constantly over low heat, cook two minutes. Increase heat to high and bring mixture to a rolling boil. Stir in liquid pectin.

Stirring constantly, bring to a rolling boil again and boil one minute. Remove from heat;skim off foam. Pour into heat resistant jars with lids. Makes about 3 pints of jam.

Blaeberry Jam

2 lb blaeberries (AKA Bilberries, Whortleberries, Blueberries, Huckleberries)
1/2 lb rhubarb
2 lb preserving sugar
MAKES 3 LB

Wash, trim and roughly chop the rhubarb, put it into a pan and cook gently until it starts to soften. Stir in the sugar and when it has dissolved add the blaeberries and bring the jam to the boil. Boil it rapidly for up to 20 minutes to setting point. Cool slightly then pour into clean warm jars, cover, label and store. (Test for setting point: test the jam by placing a spoonful on a plate, letting it cool and then pushing the surface with your finger: if it wrinkles the jam is ready)

Cherry and Raspberry Jam

1 1/2 liter sweet cherries
50 ml orange juice
25 ml lemon rind
15 ml grated orange rind
1 1/2 liter raspberries
1 liter sugar
1 a few drops almond extract

Pit and chop cherries. Add next three ingredients. Bring to boil and cook for 10 minutes, stirring frequently. Add raspberries and sugar.

Bring to a boil, stirring frequently. Boil to jam stage (15 minutes or so). Remove from heat, stir and skim for 5 minutes. Pour into hot, sterile jars and seal.

Apricot Lite Jam

2 cup (480 ml) dried apricots
1 1/2 cup (360 ml) crushed pineapple, unsweetened (if using canned, 1 drain)
1 orange, peeled, seeded and chopped 1 juice of 1/2 lemon
3 1/2 cup (840 ml) sugar

Cover apricots with cold water and let soak overnight.

Simmer apricots in soaking water, uncovered, until tender. Mash with a potato masher or in a food processor. Add pineapple, orange, lemon juice, and sugar to apricot mixture. Simmer until sugar has dissolved, stirring frequently; then cook over high heat until thick, about 20 - 30 minutes. Skim off foam. Pour into hot jars, leaving 1/4" (6mm) head space. Adjust caps.

Process 10 minutes in boiling water bath. Yield: 6 half pints (1440 mL)

Apricot Preserve

4 kg pitted, very ripe apricots (8 lbs 1; 2 oz) 3 1/4 kg sugar (7 lbs)
1 juice of 1 lemon
1 1/2 pkg einsiedehilfe ('preserving aid') dissolved in hot water

Cook apricots and sugar to setting point, continually skimming off foam.
Shortly before done, add lemon juice. Remove from heat. Stir in 'Preserving Aid'
dissolved in hot water. Pour into hot, dry, sterilized jars. Seal jars with cellophane
the top of which has been dipped in rum andsmooth the overhang over the jars'
necks, tying with thin twine.

Makes 12 half-liter jars and one quarter-liter jar. (Between 13 and 14
1 pint jars).

"Einsiedehilfe" ('Preserving Aid') is sold (in Austria) in 15 gram packages and
consists of 65 percent sugar and 35 percent benzoic acid.

To test for setting point: Spoon a little of the conserve onto a chilled saucer.
Leave for a few minutes - then hold saucer upside down. If conservedoesn't run,
then setting point has been reached.

Apricot-Raspberry Jam

2 lb apricots; peeled, pitted, and mashe 1 pint raspberries: (2 cups), mashed
6 cup sugar
1/4 cup lemon juice
1 tablespoon butter or margarine
3 oz liquid fruit pectin; 1 pouch

In a large saucepan, combine the apricots and raspberries. Stir in the sugar,
lemon juice, and butter. Bring to a boil, over high heat, stirring constantly. Add
the pectin. Bring to a rolling boil and boil for 1 minute, stirring constantly. Spoon
into jars prepared for cooked jam.
YIELD: 7 Eight Ounce Jars

Blackberry Jam

3 cup blackberries
2 cup water
1 pkg powdered fruit pectin
5 cup sugar

Crush fruit thoroughly. Add water and fruit pectin. Stir until pectin is dissolved. Heat to boiling. Boil 5-10 minutes. Add sugar. Stir until dissolved. Boil 3-5 minutes, stirring frequently, or until thick.

Blackberry Preserve

1 lb blackberries
1 lb sugar
2 tablespoon lemon juice

COMBINE ALL INGREDIENTS and let sit, covered, for 1 hour. Place in a pot, place over medium heat and cook until the mixture bubbles and thickens.
Strain through a large strainer to remove the seeds. Follow manufacturer's directions for canning, or place in jars and store in the refrigerator.

Blueberry Or Huckleberry Jam

4 1/2 cup berries
1 bottle fruit pectin
7 cup sugar
1 lemon

Wash fruit thoroughly. Crush. Add lemon juice. Add grated rind of 1/2 lemon. Add sugar. Mix thoroughly. Heat rapidly to full rolling boil.
Stir constantly before and while boiling. Boil hard 2 minutes. Remove from fire and stir in fruit pectin. Skim.

Blueberry-Cherry Jam

3 1/2 cup prepared fruit (about 1 pint fully; ripe blueberries 1 and 1 1/2 lbs fully ripe sour cherr; ies) 4 cup sugar
1 box sure-jell fruit pectin

Thoroughly crush blueberries, one layer at a time. Stem and pit sour cherries and finely chop. Combine fruits and measure 3 1/2 cups into 6-to 8-quart saucepot. Measure sugar and set aside. Mix fruit pectin into fruit in saucepot.
Place over high heat and stir u ntil mixture comes to a full boil.

Immediately add all sugar and stir. Bring to a full rolling boil and boil 1 minute, stirring constantly. Remove from heat and skim off foam with metal spoon. Ladle quickly into hot jars, filling within 1/8 inch of tops.

Wipe jar rims and threads. Cover with two-piece lids. Screw bands tightly. Invert jars for 5 minutes, then turn upright. After 1 hour, check seals.*
*Or follow water bath method recommended by USDA.
Makes 5 (1 cup) jars

Blueberry-Lemon Jam

4 1/2 cup blueberries; fresh or frozen 7 cup sugar
1 x grated zest of 2 large lemon
3 each 3-oz pouches liquid pectin

Pick over the fresh blueberries to remove any stalks and rinse under cold water. Drain well and place in a large heavy-bottomed saucepan. (Do not rinse or thaw the frozen berries.) Crush the berries slightly with a potato masher or pestle. Stir in the sugar, lemon juice, and zest. Bring to a boil over medium-high heat, stirring often. When the mixture reaches a full boil, cook for 1 minute. Stir in the pectin. Return to a ful boil, then cook for another minute. Ladle into hot, sterilized jars leaving 1/4 inch of headroom. Wipe the rims clean and put the lids on top of the jars. Process in a boiling water bath for about 5 minutes.

Remove from the water and cool completely at room temperature. Makes about 6 cups.

Blueberry-Rhubarb Jam

8 cup blueberries
4 cup rhubarb, chopped in 1 inch pieces 1 teaspoon lemon rind, grated
2 tablespoon lemon juice
1 cup water
4 cup granulated sugar

In a large heavy saucepan, combine blueberries, rhubarb, lemon rind and juice and water. Bring to a boil, stirring frequently, reduce heat and simmer, very gently, for 10 minutes. Stir in sugar; increase heat to high and boil vigorously until jam reaches setting point. (218 - 220F or 103 - 104C), 10 to 15 minutes, stirring frequently. Remove from heat, skim off foam and stir for 3 - 5 minutes to suspend fruit evenly throughout jam.

Fill sterilized jars and seal. Makes about 4 pint jars or 8 - half pint jars.

Carrot Jam

4 cup chopped carrots
3 cup sugar
3 lemons, sliced
1 teaspoon cinnamon
1/2 teaspoon cloves

Combine ingredients. Simmer slowly, stirring constantly, until thick.

Cherry Jam

4 cup sweet cherries
3 cup warmed sugar

Stone cherries. Crush the fruit. Boil in their juice till tender, about 10 minutes. Add sugar, stir well to dissolve. Boil for another 5 to 7 minutes. Remove from heat and let stand, covered, for 2 to 3 minutes. Stir and skim if necessary. Pour into sterile jars and seal.

Cherry And Raspberry Jam

1 1/2 liter sweet cherries
50 ml orange juice
25 ml lemon rind
15 ml grated orange rind
1 1/2 liter raspberries
1 liter sugar
1 a few drops almond extract

Pit and chop cherries. Add next three ingredients. Bring to boil and cook for 10 minutes, stirring frequently. Add raspberries and sugar. Bring to a boil, stirring frequently. Boil to jam stage (15 minutes or so). Remove from heat, stir and skim for 5 minutes. Pour into hot, sterile jars and seal.

Cherry Freezer Jam

1 1/2 lb sweet cherries
2 tablespoon lemon juice
4 1/4 cup sugar
1 sure jell pectin
3/4 cup water

Remove stem and pits from cherries. Finely chop in 1/8 inch pieces ending up with (2)cups of prepared cherries. Combine fruit, lemon juice and sugar in a bowl. Set aside for 10 minutes. Mix water and the sure jell together in small saucepan. Bring mixture to a boil over HIGH heat, stirring constantly.

Continue boiling for 1 minute. Stir constantly for 3 more minutes. Pour into Freezer containers, cover with lids and al ow to stand at room temperature for 24 hours. Store in freezer. After opening, store in refrigerator up to 3 weeks.

Cooked Strawberry Jam

3 quart strawberries
1/4 cup lemon juice
2 oz powdered pectin
8 1/2 cup sugar
1/4 teaspoon butter

1. Wash, hull and halve berries. Crush one layer at a time and measure 53/4 cup into a 6-quart kettle. Stir in lemon juice. Add pkg of pectin andstir thoroughly to dissolve. This will take several minutes. Stir down sides of pan and crush any remaining lumps of pectin.

2. Place pan on high heat. Bring to a boil, stirring constantly to prevent scorching.

3. Add sugar gradually, then butter, mixing well. Continue stirring and bring to a full rolling boil (a boil that cannot be stirred down). Boil hard exactly 4 minutes, stirring constantly to prevent scorching.

4. Remove jam from heat. Skim foam from top.

5. Pour into hot, sterilized jars, wipe top and threads of jar. Apply hot lid and screw band. Twist screw band down tight. Process in boiling water bath 5 minutes. Start counting time when water comes to a boil.

Green Tomato Jam

1 kg green tomatoes
1 each lemon
1 cup water
3 cup sugar

Slice tomatoes and lemon thinly. Put tomatoes, lemon and sugar into a pot with the water. Bring to a boil, reduce heat and simmer for 1 hour. Transfer to a warmed sterile jars.

Fig Jam

2 quart chopped figs, about 5 lbs
6 cup sugar
3/4 cup water
1/4 cup lemon juice

To prepare chopped figs, cover figs with boiling water. Let stand 10 minutes. Drain, stem and chop figs.

Combine figs, sugar, and 3/4 c. water in a large sauce pot. Bring slowly to a boil, stirring until sugar dissolves. Cook rapidly until thick. Stir frequently to prevent sticking. Add lemon juice and cook 1 minute longer.

Pour hot into hot jars, leaving 1/4" head space. Adjust caps. Process 15 minutes in boiling water bath.
Yield: About 5 pints

Framboise Raspberry Jam

4 1/2 cup fresh raspberries
3 cup sugar
1/4 cup framboise

Servings: makes 4 - 1/2 pint jars Notes: The combination of the delicacy of fresh raspberries and the mellow framboise (raspberry brandy) makes a remarkable jam. Use both as a spread and as a dessert garnish.

DIRECTIONS: Place all ingredients in heavy saucepan over medium heat. Bring to a boil, stirring occasionally. When mixture comes to a boil, raise heat to high and cook, stirring constantly, for about 20 minutes. As mixture begins to thicken, watch carefully to prevent sticking. When mixture has reached a jam like consistency, immediately remove from heat.

Pour into hot sterilized jars and vacuum seal (hot water bath method, or can be refrigerated up to 6 weeks).

Honeyed Peach Preserve

3 lb peaches, peeled and quartered
4 cup sugar
1 cup honey
1/2 orange, quartered
1/2 teaspoon salt
1/4 teaspoon almond extract

Combine peaches, sugar, and honey in Dutch oven. Cover and let stand for 45 minutes. Position knife blade in food processor bowl. Add orange, and top with cover. Process until finely chopped. Measure chopped orange, and add an equal amount of water. Cook covered, about 10 minutes or until orange peel is soft. Set aside. Bring peaches slowly to a boil, stirring frequently until sugar dissolves. Bring to a rapid boil, and cook 15 minutes, stirring constantly. Add orange mixture, return to a boil, and cook about 25 minutes or until mixture registers 221 degrees on candy thermometer; stir mixture frequently.

Mango Jam

4 cup mango pulp (buy about 6 lb)
1/4 cup lemon juice
6 cup sugar
1 pkg dry pectin

Wash fruit, peel, seed and cut in cubes. Mash with a potato masher or run through a food processor or blender - try NOT to puree. In a 10 qt pan, mix fruit, lemon juice and pectin. Place over high heat; stirring constantly, bring to a rolling boil that cannot be stirred down. Still stirring, add sugar. Return to a boil that cannot be stirred down, then boil for exactly 2 minutes. Remove from heat; skim off foam. Ladle hot jam into prepared half-pint jars. Wipe rims clean. Place lids on jars and firmly screw on rings. Process in boiling water bath for ten minutes. Makes about 6 1/2 cups.

Kiwi Daiquiri Jam

5 kiwifruit, peeled
3 cup sugar
2/3 cup unsweetened pineapple juice
1/3 cup fresh lime juice
1 pouch 85ml/3oz liquid pectin
1 green food colour, optional
4 tablespoon rum (or sub. fruit juice?)

Fill boiling water canner with water. Place 4 clean half-pint mason jars in canner. Cover, bring water to a boil; boil at least 10 min to sterilize jars at altitudes up to 1000 ft.

Place snap lids in boiling water, boil 5 min to soften sealing compound.
In a large stainless steel or enamel saucepan, mash kiwifruit to applesauce consistency. Stir in sugar, pineapple and lime juice. Bring to a full rolling boil, stirring until sugar dissolves. Stirring constantly, boil vigorously for 2 minutes. Remove from heat, stir in pectin. Continue stirring 5 minutes to prevent floating fruit. (If desired, add green food coloring to create a more lively, intensely green jam.) Stir in rum.

Ladle jam into a hot sterilized jar to within 1/4 inch of top rim. Remove air bubbles by sliding rubber spatula between glass and food; readjust head space to 1/4 inch. Wipe jar rim removing any stickiness. Center snap lid on jar; apply screw band just until fingertip tight. Place jar in canner. Repeat for remaining jam.

Cover canner, return water to a boil, process 5 minutes at altitudes up to 1000 ft. Remove jars. Cool 24 hours. Check jar seals. (Sealed lids curve downward.) Remove screw bands. Wipe jars, label and store in a cool dark place.

Low-Sugar Refrigerator Strawberry Jam

4 cup sliced strawberries
1/3 cup sugar
2 tablespoon lemon juice
1 envelope unflavored gelatin
1/2 cup water

1. In a medium saucepan, combine strawberries, sugar and lemon juice. Heat 5 minutes, crushing the berries slightly. Bring to a boil; boll rapidly, stirring constantly, 3 minutes.

2. In a smal bowl, sprinkle unflavored gelatin over cold water. Let stand 1 minute. Add to strawberry mixture and heat, stirring until gelatin is completely dissolved, about 3 minutes.

3. Let jam stand 5 minutes, skiing off foam with a spoon. Ladle into jars. Cover and cool slightly before storing in the refrigerator for several weeks or in the freezer for longer storage.

If cooked jam does not set 24 hours after processing there are steps that can be taken to solve the problem. The Department of Agriculture Home and Garden Bulletin No. 56 states: Soft jams made with regular pectin can sometimes be improved by recooking according to the following directions. It is best to recook only 4 to 6 cup of jelly or jam at one time.

To remake with powdered pectin: Measure the jam to be recooked. For each quart of jelly or jam, measure 1/@ cup sugar, ¼ cup water and 4 tsp powdered pectin. Mix the pectin and water and bring to boiling, stirring constantly to prevent scorching. Add the jam and sugar. Stir thoroughly. Bring to a full rolling boil over high heat, stirring constantly. Boil mixture hard for 1/2 minute. Remove jam from the heat; skim off foam. Ladle into hot sterilized jars. Adjust lids and screw bands and process in a boiling water bath for 5 minutes. Start counting time when water comes to a boil.

To remake with liquid pectin: Measure the jam to be recooked. For each quart of jam, measure 3/4 cup sugar, 2 Tbsp lemon juice and 2 Tbsp liquid pectin. Bring jam to boiling over high heat. Quickly add the sugar, lemon juice and pectin and bring to a full rolling boil; stir constantly. Boil mixture hard for 1 minute. Remove jam from the heat; skim off foam. Ladle into hot sterilized jars. Adjust lids and screw bands and process in a boiling water bath for 5 minutes. Start counting time when water comes to a boil.

Microwave Cherry Preserve

3 cup pitted red cherries
1 cup water
2 teaspoon lemon juice
3 cup sugar
1/4 cup powdered pectin
1/2 teaspoon almond extract

Combine cherries, water, lemon juice and pectin in a 3-quart, microwave safe bowl. Cover with plastic wrap or waxed paper and bring to a boil in the microwave oven on high setting (about 8 minutes). Remove from the oven and stir in remaining ingredients. Cover; place in the microwave oven; and return to a boil on high setting (about 6 minutes). Stir and return to microwave, uncovered. Cook 3 minutes. Stir and return to microwave oven, uncovered. Cook 3 minutes or until preserves sheet from spoon.
Remove from oven; skim foam if necessary. Pour hot into hot jars, leaving 1/4 inch head space. Adjust caps. Process 10 minutes in boiling water bath. Do not attempt to process in microwave oven. Yield: about 3 half pints.

Microwave Jam

Prepare specific fruit as directed below. Place in a 3-quart casserole.
Add specific amount of sugar, butter, lemon juice and flavoring. Cook, UNCOVERED, on high about 15 minutes, boiling. Boil ONLY 2 minutes. Test again.

STRAWBERRY JAM: Crush about 3 1/2 cups of whole berries to make 2 cups. Add: 1 1/2 cups sugar, 1/2 teaspoon butter, 1 1/2 tablespoons lemon juice. Cook as above.
RASPBERRY JAM: 3 cups berries to make 2 cups fruit. Add 1 1/2 sugar, 1/2 t. butter, 1 T. lemon juice.
BLUEBERRY JAM: SLIGHTLY crush about 3 cups berries to make 2 cups. 1 12/ C. sugar, 1/2 t. butter: 1/4 c. lemon juice, 1/2 t. grated lemon peel and
SWEET CHERRY JAM: Remove pits from 1 lb. of fruit. Cut in quarters to make 2 cups. Add 1 1/2 C. sugar, 1/2 t. butter, 1/4 C. lemon juice, 1/2 t. grated lemon peel, a 2-inch cinnamon stick after cooking.
PLUM JAM: Remove pits and chop about 1 lb. plums to make 2 cups. Add 1 1/2 cups sugar, 1/2 t. butter, 1 T. lemon juice.
Al these are to be cooked as above.

Microwave Strawberry Jam

1 cup crushed strawberries
2 teaspoon lemon juice
3/4 cup sugar
1/4 teaspoon butter

1. Stir together strawberries, lemon juice, sugar and butter in an 8-cup microwave-safe measuring cup.
2. Microwave on 100 percent power for 4 minutes, then stir and continue to microwave at 100 percent power for 4 minutes. Pour into covered container, cool and refrigerate.

Mrs. Johnson's Peach Preserve

4 cup sugar
1 cup water
1 tablespoon lemon extract
6 lb (around 24) ripe peaches, peeled an;d sliced

1. In a large saucepan, dissolve sugar in water over medium-high heat and bring to a boil; cook for about 5 minutes, or until syrup is clear.
Skim off any froth.

2. Add vanilla and lemon extract, stir in peaches, and return to a boil. Watch carefully to prevent from boiling over.

3. Boil for 5 minutes. Remove from heat and skim off any froth.

4. Fill hot, sterilized jars (quart-size screw-top Mason jars) and adjust caps; a suction seal will form with cooling. Store in a cool, dark place. Serve with hot biscuits, or warm over vanilla or Texas peach ice cream.
Makes 3 quarts.

Nectarine And Raspberry Preserve

6 lb large nectarines unpeeled
1 and sliced) - 8 cups
3 cup sugar
2 tablespoon fresh lemon juice
2 cup raspberries (1 pint)

Combine the nectarines with the sugar and lemon juice and let stand, covered, overnight in the refrigerator.
Place a colander in a large shallow preserving pan and pour in the nectarine mixture. Let the juices drip into the pan for at least 30
minutes. Remove the colander with the fruit to a bowl and bring the juices in the pan to a boil over high heat. Boil rapidly for 20 to 30
minutes, or until reduced by half. Add the nectarines and any additional juices to the syrup in the pan and continue to cook over high heat for 10
minutes.
Carefully stir in the raspberries and cook for 5 minutes more. The nectarines will look lightly glazed and the syrup will be only slightly thickened. Ladle the preserves into hot sterilized jars, wipe the rims clean with a damp towel, and seal with new lids and metal rings. Process in hot-water bath for 5 minutes. Remove, cool, check seals, label, and store.
Makes 8 half-pint jars.

Freezer Strawberry Jam

1 quart ripe strawberries
4 cup sugar
2 tablespoon lemon juice
1/2 each bottle of liquid pectin

Crush berries thoroughly. Place in a large bowl. Add sugar, mix well and let stand. Mix lemon juice and add certo. Stir until all sugar crystals are dissolved. Ladle quickly into jars and leave to set, it may take 24 hours. Store in freezer. Will keep in the fridge for 3 weeks.

Freezer Strawberry Jam 2

1 quart ripe strawberries
4 cup sugar
2 tablespoon lemon juice
1/2 bottle of liquid pectin

Crush berries thoroughly. Place in a large bowl. Add sugar, mix well and let stand. Mix lemon juice and add certo. Stir until all sugar crystals are dissolved. Ladle quickly into jars and leave to set, it may take 24 hours. Store in freezer. Will keep in the fridge for 3 weeks.

No Cook Blueberry Strawberry Jam

1 cup strawberries, crushed
2 cup blueberries, fresh or frozen crushed 5 cup sugar
2 tablespoon lemon juice
2 pkg certo liquid (2 pouches)

Measure prepared fruit into a large bowl. Add sugar to fruit and mix well. Let stand for 10 minutes. Stir in Certo Liquid Fruit Pectin and lemon juice. Continue to stir for 3 minutes until most of the sugar is dissolved. Pour into clean jars or plastic containers and cover tightly with lids. Let stand at room temperature until set, up to 24 hours. Store in freezer or up to 3 weeks in frig. Makes 7 cups.

Mock Strawberry or Raspberry Jam

6 cup mashed figs
6 cup sugar
1 cup water
9 oz strawberry or raspberry jello

Boil hard for 3 minutes. Put in hot, clean jelly jars and seal. Let set 6weeks and enjoy.

No Cook Peachy Orange Jam

1 orange
2 1/2 cup peaches, finely chopped
1/3 cup maraschino cherries, chopped
2 tablespoon lemon juice
5 cup sugar
3/4 cup water
1 pkg certo fruit pectin crystals

Grate orange rind. Section orange, remove membrane. Dice sections and put into a large bowl with rind. Add peaches, cherries, lemon juice and sugar. Mix well. Let stand 10 minutes.

Combine water and Certo in a small saucepan. Boil for 1 minute, stirring constantly.
Stir pectin into fruit mixture for 3 minutes until most of sugar is dissolved.
Pour into clean jars or plastic containers. Cover tightly with lids and let stand at room temperature til set. (may take 24 hours) Store in freezer or for 3 weeks in frig. Makes 6 1/2 cups

No Cook Strawberry Kiwi Jam

2 3/4 cup crushed strawberries
1 1/4 cup peeled, chopped kiwi fruit
3 1/4 cup sugar
1 box fruit pectin crystals

Measure prepared fruits into a large bowl. Measure sugar and set aside. Combine Pectin crystals with 1/4 cup of the measured sugar. Gradually add to fruit, stirring well. Let stand for 30 minutes, stirring occasionally.

Stir in remaining sugar and continue to stir for 3 minutes until most of the sugar is dissolved. Pour into clean jars or plastic containers. Cover with tight lids and let stand at room temperature until set (may take up to24 hours) Store in freezer or for 3 weeks in refrigerator. Makes 6 cups.

No-Cook Apple Raspberry Jam

3 cup fully ripe raspberries
1/2 cup finely ground peeled and cored appl; es 4 cup sugar
2 tablespoon fresh lemon juice
1 pouch liquid fruit pectin
Thoroughly crush the berries, using a potato masher, sieve half of the pulp to remove some of the seeds, if desired; measure 1-1/2 cups of prepared berries; pour into a large bowl. Add apples. Add sugar to bowl; mix well;let stand 10 minutes. Add lemon juice and liquid fruit pectin to bowl; stir for 3 minutes. (A few sugar crystals will remain) Ladle jam into clean containers, leaving 1/4 inch head space; cover with tight fitting lids; let stand at room temperature until set (may take up to 24 hours) store in freezer. Jam can be stored in the refrigerator if used within 3 weeks.

Makes 4-1/2 cups.

No-Cook Georgia Peachberry Jam

1 cup raspberries, crushed
1 cup peaches, peeled and finely chopped 3 3/4 cup sugar
2 tablespoon lemon juice
1 certo liquid pouch
Measure prepared fruits into a large bowl.

Add sugar to fruit and mix well. Let stand 10 minutes.
Stir in Certo liquid Fruit Pectin and lemon juice. Continue to stir for 3 minutes until most of the sugar is dissolved.

Pour into clean jars or plastic containers. Cover tightly with lids and let stand at room temperature until set (may take 24 hours) Store in freezer or for 3 weeks in fridge. Makes 4 1/2 cups

No-Cook Light Bananaberry Jam

3 cup crushed strawberries
1 cup mashed banana
3 cup sugar

1 box certo light fruit pectin crystals Measure fruits into a large bowl. Measure sugar and set aside. Combine CERTO fruit pectin crystals with 1/4 cup of the measured sugar. Gradually add to fruit, stirring well. Let stand for 30 minutes, stirring occasionally. Gradually stir in remaining sugar and continue stirring for 3 minutes until most of the sugar is dissolved. Pour into clean jars or plastic containers. Cover tightly with lids. let stand at room temperature until set (may take up to 24 hours). Store in freezer or up to 3 weeks in fridge.

Makes 6 cups.

No-Cook Peach Jam

1 lb peaches: peeled, pitted and mashed,; 2 cups 2 cup sugar
3 oz liquid fruit pectin; 1 pouch
2 tablespoon lemon juice

Stir the mashed peaches and sugar together in a large bowl, blending well, and let stand 10 minutes, stirring occasionally. Add the liquid fruit pectin and lemon juice. Stir, constantly, for 3 minutes. Spoon into jars prepared for freezer jams. YIELD: 3 Eight Ounce Jars

Mock Raspberry Jam

5 cup green tomatoes
4 cup sugar
6 oz raspberry jello (2 pkgs)

In blender or processor, process green tomatoes; add sugar. Boil 20 minutes. Skim. Add jello, stir. Pour into sterilized jars. It must be kept in the refrigerator! Can also be frozen.

No-Cook Strawberry Freezer Jam

1 3/4 quart fully ripe strawberries
1 3/4 cup sugar
1 pkg sure-jell light fruit pectin
1 cup corn syrup

1. Hull and thoroughly crush strawberries, one layer at a time. Measure into a large bowl. You should have 4 cups.

2. Measure sugar. Combine fruit pectin with 1/4 cup of the sugar. Gradually add pectin mixture to fruit, stirring vigorously.

3. Set aside for 30 minutes, stirring occasionally. Add corn syrup; mix well. Gradually stir in remaining sugar until dissolved. Ladle quickly into scalded containers. Cover at once with tight lids. Let stand overnight, then store in freezer. Small amounts may be covered and stored in refrigerator up to 3 weeks.

No-Cook Strawberry Jam

1 pint strawberries; (2 cups) mashed
2 cup sugar
3 oz liquid pectin; 1 pouch
2 tablespoon lemon juice
3 drop red food coloring; up to 4 drops may be used

Stir the berries and sugar together in a large bowl, blending well, and let stand for 10 minutes, stirring occasionally. Add the pectin, lemon juice and food coloring, blending wel , and stir constantly for 3 minutes.
Spoon the jam into the jars prepared for freezer jams.

YIELD: 3 Eight Ounce Jars

Peach Jam

4 cup prepared fruit
1 bottle fruit pectin
7 1/2 cup sugar

Peel peaches. Pit, and grind or crush. If peaches lack flavor, add juice of 1 lemon. Combine sugar and fruit. Heat rapidly to full rolling boil.

Stir constantly before and while boiling. Boil hard 1 minute. Remove from fire. Stir in fruit pectin. Skim and stir alternately for 5 minutes to cool jam slightly and to prevent floating fruit.

Peach Preserve

2 lb peaches
3 cup sugar
1/2 cup water

Peel peaches. Remove pits. Cut each peach in 6 or 8 pieces. Combine sugar and water. Boil 5 minutes. Add fruit. Boil slowly until fruit is clear and juice is thick.

Peach Rhubarb Jam

2 qt. sliced or fresh rhubarb, 1 inch; pieces 4 cup sugar
1 can peach pie filling (21 oz.)
1 pkg orange flavored gelatin

In a large bowl, combine rhubarb and sugar; allow to stand over night. Transfer to a large saucepan and bring to a boil. Reduce heat and simmer for 10 minutes. Meanwhile, dice peaches and add with filling to saucepan; return to boiling. Remove from heat; add gelatin and stir until dissolved. Spoon into canning jars or freezer containers. Cool completely.
Refrigerate or freeze. Yield: About 7 half-pints

Pineapple Apricot Jam

2 lb dried apricots
2 cup crushed pineapple
3 1/4 cup sugar

Wash apricots. Cover with cold water. Heat slowly to boiling. Simmer until soft. Add pineapple and sugar. Simmer slowly, stirring frequently, until thick.

Pumpkin Jam

5 lb pumpkin
1 lb raisins
1 lb dried apricots
2 1/2 lb sugar

Pare pumpkin. Remove seeds and cut pulp into cubes. Add sugar. Stir well,and allow to stand overnight. In the morning add apricots which have been washed and cut in strips. Add raisins. Cook slowly, stirring frequently, until the pumpkin is tender and clear. One-half a lemon, sliced thinly, maybe added. Canned pumpkin may be substituted for fresh pumpkin.

Pumpkin Preserve

4 lb pumpkin (prepared)
3 lemons
4 lb sugar
1/2 teaspoon salt
1 tablespoon mixed spices *

Wash pumpkin. Remove peel and seed. Cut pumpkin as wanted. Weigh and mix with sugar. let stand 12 to 18 hours in a cool place. Add thinly sliced lemons, salt and mixed spices (tied in bag). Boil until pumpkin is clear and syrup thick. Pour, boiling hot, into hot Ball jars; seal at once.
*NOTE: Use ginger, nutmeg, cinnamon, etc to flavor this your way.

Rhubarb And Fig Preserve

3 1/2 quart rhubarb
1 pint chopped figs
8 cup sugar
1 lemon

Cut rhubarb into small pieces, add sugar and let mixture stand overnight.
In the morning, boil until thick and add 1 pint of chopped figs plus the juice and rind of 1 lemon. Cook rapidly until mixture is thick and clear.
Pack while hot into sterile, hot jars. Seal immediately.

Rhubarb-Strawberry-Jam

1 quart fresh strawberries
1 lb rhubarb
1/4 cup water
6 1/2 cup sugar
1 pouch liquid pectin

1. Remove caps from strawberries. Crush berries, one layer at a time.
Trim (do not peel) rhubarb. Thinly slice or chop stalks. Add water.
Cover and simmer 2 minutes or until soft. Add to the prepared strawberries.
2. Measure 3 1/2 cup of prepared fruit. If it measures slightly less, add water.
Place measured fruit in a 6 or 8-quart saucepan.
3. Measure sugar exactly and set aside. Open liquid pectin and set the pouch upright in a cup.
4. Stir sugar into prepared fruit. The saucepan must be no more than one-third full to allow for a full rolling boil.
5. Bring to a full rolling boil over high heat. Boil hard 1 minute, stirring constantly. Remove from heat.
6. Stir in pectin at once. Quickly skim off foam with a large metal spoon.
Immediately ladle into hot jars, leaving 1/4-inch space at top. With a damp cloth, wipe jar rims and threads clean.
7. Immediately cover jars with hot canning lids. Screw bands on firmly.
8. Place jars in a boiling water bath, carefully setting jars on rack in canner of boiling water. Cover canner and return water to a boil; boil 5 minutes.
9. Remove jars from canner and let cool. Check seals and store in a cool, dry place.

Sweet Banana Jam

2 cup mashed banana
2 tablespoon lemon juice

Blend ingredients together until smooth. Heat to a boil in a saucepan; turn to low and simmer, stirring occasionally, until mixture thickens.
Yields 1/3 cup.

Ripe Grape Jam

4 1/2 cup prepared ripened grapes
1/2 cup water
7 cup sugar
1/2 bottle fruit pectin

Use only fully-ripened grapes. Separate skins and pulp. Simmer pulp 5 minutes. Remove seeds by sieving. Crush skins. Add pulp. Add water and stir until mixture boils. Cover, and simmer slowly 30 minutes. Measure fruit into large kettle. Add sugar. Mix well. Heat rapidly to full rolling boil. Stir constantly before and while boiling. Boil hard 1 minute.
Remove from fire. Stir in fruit pectin. Skim.

Red Raspberry Jam

3 cup finely mashed or sieved red raspberries 6 cup sugar
1 pkg powdered pectin
1 cup water

Combine berries and sugar. Let stand about 20 minutes, stirring occasionally. Combine pectin and water in a small saucepan. Bring to a boil; boil 1 minute, stirring constantly. Add pectin to fruit mixture; stir 3 minutes. Pour into can or freeze jars, leaving 1/2 inch head space. Adjust caps. Let stand until set, up to 24 hours. Freeze. Yield: about 9 half pints.

Spiced Cherry Orange Jam

4 oranges
1 water
2 sticks cinnamon
4 whole allspice
6 whole cloves
4 lb fresh dark sweet cherries, pitted 1/2 cup fresh lemon juice
6 1/2 cup sugar

Slice oranges very thinly; place in preserving kettle; add water to cover by 1/4 inch, about 5 cups. Tie spices in a cheesecloth bag; add to kettle;bring to boil over high heat; reduce heat slightly; boil until oranges are very tender; remove spice bag and discard. Add pitted cherries, lemon juice, and sugar to kettle; stir until sugar is dissolved; return mixture to boil; boil rapidly until mixture thickens and reaches gel stage, about 1hour. Cool for about 5 minutes, skimming off foam with a metal spoon and stirring occasionally. Ladle into hot sterilized jars, leaving 1/2 inch head space; seal with melted paraffin wax; cover with clean lids. Store in a cool, dark, dry place.

Makes 11 1/2 pint jars.

Ripe Tomato Jam

4 lb medium ripe tomatoes
4 cup sugar
1 teaspoon whole cloves
1/2 tablespoon broken stick cinnamon
2 cup vinegar
1/2 teaspoon whole allspice

Scald, peel, and quarter tomatoes. Place in preserving kettle. Add sugar, vinegar, cloves, allspice, and cinnamon. The spices may be tied in a loose muslin bag. Simmer, stirring frequently, until thick.

Strawberry and Apple Jam

500 gm strawberries
3 large green apples
1/4 cup lemon juice
2 cup water
1 kg sugar, warmed

Wash, hull and half the strawberries. Peel, core and quarter the apples. Ten cut quarters into thin slices. Put al the ingredients, except the sugar, into a large pot. Cover and bring to a boil. Simmer until the fruit is tender. Add warmed sugar and stir till it has dissolved. Increase heat, stirring frequently and cook till setting point is reached.

Remove from heat and let stand for 5 minutes. Pour into warm sterile jars and seal.

Strawberry Liqueur Jam

500 gm strawberries
1 medium green apple
1 juice of 1 lime
1 3/4 cup sugar
2 tablespoon grand marnier

Wash and hul strawberries. Peel, core and finely chop apple. Add lime juice and let stand covered for 30 minutes. Microwave the fruit and juice for 4 minutes on high. Add sugar, stir and microwave 35 minutes on high, stirring every 10 minutes. Stand five minutes, pour into warm sterile jars. Seal.

Strawberry-Kiwi Jam

2 3/4 cup crushed strawberries
1 1/4 cup kiwi fruit, peeled, chopped 3 1/4 cup sugar
1 pkg certo light pectin crystals

Measure prepared fruits into a large bowl. Measure sugar and set aside. Combine Certo Light Fruit Pectin Crystals (no substitute) with 1/4 cup of the measured sugar. Gradually add to fruit, stirring well.

Let stand 30 min, stirring occasionally. Stir in remaining sugar and continue to stir for 3 minutes until most of the sugar is dissolved.

Pour into clean jars or plastic containers. Cover with tight lids and let stand at room temperature until set (may take up to 24 hours).

Store in freezer or for 3 weeks in refrigerator. Makes 6 cups.

Tomato Jam

1 1/2 kg tomatoes
100 gm glace pineapple
1 each green apple
1 tablespoon grated lemon rind
1/2 cup lemon juice
3 1/2 cup sugar

Peel and coarsely chop tomatoes. Coarsely chop pineapple. Peel, core and grate apple. Combine the fruit in a large pot. Bring to a boil, simmer uncovered for 20 minutes. Stir in lemon juice.

Add sugar and stir till dissolved. Boil rapidly, uncovered, for 45 minutes or until a setting point is reached. Remove from heat and stand for 5 minutes. Pour into warm sterile jars and seal.

Zucchini Jam

6 cup zucchini-peeled and grated
1/4 cup water
1 pkg sure-jell
5 cup sugar
13 oz crushed pineapple
6 oz apricot jello

Boil the zucchini and water until soft. Add Sure-Jell and bring to a hard boil. Add sugar and pineapple. Boil 5 minutes. Remove form heat. Add apricot Jello. Stir well. Pack in sterilized jars and seal.

I use the Sure-Jell Light and use only 3 1/2 cups sugar. This is an orange colored jam and really tastes great unless you don't like apricots or pineapple!

Muscadine Habanero Jam

6 lb ripe muscadines
2 ripe habaneros, stemmed,
1 seeded for lesser heat (!)
1 plum (santa rosa or friar),
1 seed removed, for natural
1 pectin
5 cup granulated sugar
2 cup water

In a heavy saucepan combine the muscadines, chiles, plum, sugar, and water. Slightly crush the muscadines on the bottom of the pan with a potato masher. Let boil 30-40 minutes until it is thickened to a heavy syrup consistency. Remove from heat and strain mixture through a mesh strainer using a rubber spatula to press pulp through a strainer into a bowl. Discard the seed mixture. Pour the hot jam into sterilized mason jars and seal. Refrigerate a few months or hot water bath and store on shelves.

Fig Preserve (Syko Glyko)

50 small green figs
1 blanched almonds (optional)
3 cup sugar
3 cup water
1 tablespoon lemon juice

1 strip of grapefruit peel or-lemon; peel Wash figs and trim stems. Place figs in a large pan and cover with boiling water. Bring to a the boil and boil gently, uncovered, for 15 minutes. Drain and rinse with hot water. Return to pan and cover again with boiling water. Repeat boiling and draining process four times in all. Cook until figs are tender after last change of water (about 1 hour's cooking in all).

Drain figs, rinse with cold water and spread out on paper towels to dry.
Insert a whole or split almond into base of each fig if desired.

In a clean pan bring sugar and water to the boil. Add lemon juice and grapefruit or lemon peel and boil for 10 minutes. Add figs and boil over moderate heat for 10 minutes, skimming when necessary. Cover pan and leave overnight.

Next day bring pan contents slowly to the boil and boil gently until syrup is thick when tested. Put figs and syrup into sterilised jars, seal and store in a cool place. Testing syrup: Drip a little syrup onto a cold plate. If drops do not spread, syrup is ready. If you have a sugar thermometer, cook to a temperature of 105 C (220 F).

Strawberry and Gooseberry Jam

2 quart stemmed gooseberries
2 quart hulled strawberries
4 quart sugar

Wash fruits carefully. Drain. Add sugar. Heat slowly to boiling. Simmer slowly, stirring frequently, until thick.

Apple Preserve

6 cup peeled-cored-sliced apples
1 tablespoon lemon juice
1 lemon; thinly sliced
4 cup sugar
1 cup water
1 pkg pectin
2 teaspoon ground nutmeg

This is NOT jam. I like to use these warmed as a side dish (like escalloped apples).

Mix apples, water, lemon juice in large pot. Simmer covered 10 min.

Stir in pectin and bring to full rolling boil, stir frequently. Add lemon slices/sugar and bring to full rolling boil again and boil for 1 min, stir frequently. Remove from heat and add nutmeg. Pour into hot jars or cool and put into freezer containers. If canning, process 10 min in boiling water bath. Yield 6 half pints. IF FREEZING, MAKE SURE YOU COOL FIRST, IT WILL BE HOT ENOUGH TO MELT PLASTIC !

Fruit-Sweetened Strawberry Jam

2 cup sliced fresh strawberries
1/3 cup apple-grape concentrate
1 (see separate recipe)
2 tablespoon water
2 tablespoon orange juice

1. In a medium pan combine the strawberries, apple-grape sweetener, water and orange juice. Bring to a boil, reduce the heat slightly and cook at a low boil 10 to 15 minutes, until very thick. Stir often. (To test for gelling, put about 1/2 teaspoon jam on a chilled saucer and place in freezer for 1 minute. If, when cooled, jam wrinkles when touched, it is done.) Skim the foam from the top of the jam.

2. Transfer to a bowl, cool, cover, and refrigerate.

CPSIA information can be obtained
at www.ICGtesting.com
Printed in the USA
BVHW011441160621
609530BV00007B/921